Letters to the
One-Armed Poet

Village Books Press – Cheyenne, OK

Cover Design: Merleyn Bell
Cover Photo: Nathan Brown
Back Cover Photos: Nathan and Ashley Brown

Village Books Press
Cheyenne, Oklahoma

Also by Nathan Brown:

My Sideways Heart   (2010)
Two Tables Over   (2008)
Not Exactly Job   (2007)
Suffer the Little Voices   (2005)
Ashes Over the Southwest   (2005)
Hobson's Choice   (2002)

Letters to the One-Armed Poet

❧ O ❧

A Memoir
of Friendship, Loss,
and Butternut Squash Ravioli

~ Nathan Brown ~

Table of Contents

Acknowledgements vii
Not Exactly Ulysses 2
Before ....
The Collision 4
That Trip to Ouray 6
The Hand You're Dealt 10
Cowboys & Eskimos 11
Have You Heard? 13
Hoisting the Sails at Agora 14
Trucks and Monsters 15
Unaccustomed 16
Note to Another Oklahoma Hitchhiker 17
Multiplying Cells 18
He Gave His Only 19
Human Subject Research 20
The Good Fight 22
Existential Solstice 23
After ....
Ice and Snow 26
For You to Know 27
My Good Man 28
At Your Funeral 30
The Bléssed Bones 31
Highs and Lows 32
The Only Thing Worse 33
Way to Go 34
Revenance 35
Mugs and Buckets 36
Great Plans 37
Too Late Sherlock 38
Who's in Charge Here? 39
Going over "Details" 40
Word for Word 41
Heavy Weights 42
Nip and Tuck 44

Belly Up 45
The Low-Down 46
All the Same 47
The Way... Things Go 48
Man vs. Their Nature 50
Walking Shadows 51
Back Here... 52
In the Cards 53
I'd Push the Buttons 54
The First September Without 55
The Lost Suppers ....
Bread Among Brothers 58
The Last Supper 59
The Poem that Launched a Million Calories 61
The Sacrifice 62
The Power of Velveeta 63
Why I Lick the Bowl 64
Midnight in the Garden 65
A Bottle Among Friends 66
Family Fortune 67
Deep-Fried Tradition 68
Bursting My Bubbles 69
Baking Time 70
Dr. Sushi in Nirvanaland 71
Not That I'm Old 72
Having Eggs and Options 73
B.M.S. 74
Fools and Messes 75
Cheese in the Garden of Eden 77
Sweet and Salty 78
Avocado in Three Movements 79
Strawberry and Banana 82
Flowers and Dust 83
Pearl and Red 84
An Expensive Cure 86

Ribs and Stones 88
The Story of the Day 90
Capturing the Moment 92
Sauce Man 93
Too Chany Meshiritas 94
Big Giblets 95
Wise Decision 96
This 97
In My Mother's Home Town 98
Lattes in Purgatory 99
Sin Big 100
What Brings Us Here 102
They Are the Brown Sugar of the Earth 104
No Recipes for These Territories 106
Forsooth... 107
White or Wheat 108
The Basic Ingredients 110
Never Know 112
Las Vegas: The Last Leg of the Lost Suppers ....
We'll Always Have Paris 114
Layover at the Sleeping Dog Tavern 118
Mornings with Coffee at Mon Amí... 120
The Usual Stuff... 122
Viva la Noise 125
Down 126
Up 128
Conjecture 130
...and Good Luck 132
Culmination 134
One Last Big One 136
Stepping Back 140

Acknowledgements

Many, many people were a part of this story, whether directly or indirectly. So, this will be difficult territory to cover...

To LeAnn Chastain, whose receptive heart and spirit made much of this book possible.

To those who loved Jim and supported us in our poetic endeavors in so many ways: Dorothy Alexander, Billy and Dodee Crockett, Taci Fast, Full Circle Bookstore, Ginny Jackson and Steven Raab (for their fabulous house concerts and all the bed and breakfast services rendered), Ken Hada, Carol Hamilton, Carol Koss, Charlotte Lankard, Lise Liddell, Jeanetta & Kyran Mish, Jim and Aline Spurr, Ann Thompson (and the Oklahoma Humanities Council), Beth Wood.

To those who showed for some of the *Lost Suppers*: Ashley, Dorothy Alexander, Denae Athay, Sierra Brown, Mike Bumgarner, Calvin-the-paperboy, LeAnn, Maddye, Jim & Sharon Chastain, Alan & Suzanne Cheshier, Darian Cheshier, Julie Cooper, Billy Crockett, Don Dorsey, Jim Drummond, Sandy Fuzzell, Carol Hamilton, Herb & Valerie Hampton, Kelley Hampton, Anne Harris, Jeff & Cheryl Jones, Michael & Katie Kimberling, Ginger Murray, Devey Napier, Joshua & Tiffany Nelson, Sandra Soli, Al Turner, Joshua Vaught.

To R.C. Davis-Undiano and Karla K. Morton for a careful and thoughtful read through.

Special thanks to Dorothy Alexander for her wonderful work with Village Books Press; to Merleyn Bell for her excellent design work; and to Don and Shellie Greiner for their gracious gift towards the Las Vegas project.

As always... to my parents, Norma and Lavonn Brown, whose support and encouragement appear to know no end;

to Sierra, who puts up with a dad who has such a weird and nomadic life; and especially to Ashley, who is not only tireless in her love and support, but also with her eagle-eye editing.

"Human Subject Research" and "The Only Thing Worse" appeared in *Blood and Thunder: Musings on the Art of Medicine*; "Existential Solstice" appeared in "Walt's Corner" of *The Long-Islander*. "Ice and Snow," "At Your Funeral," and "All the Same" appeared in *Windhover*.

Letters to the
One-Armed Poet

For Jim...

Not Exactly Ulysses

All this happened, more or less.

~Kurt Vonnegut

I'm afraid I've idealized our years together… the poems, performances, and the stories… as well as the fallout from all three. There is no tool in the writer's box more important than delusion.

And death often breaks out the Lemon Pledge, after everyone drives away from the funeral, and wipes the fingerprints off of what actually happened… puts a nice reflective shine on the surface of things.

But in the last couple of years, you often worried, on some of the darker days, about how you'd be remembered—or even to what extent you'd be remembered at all.

And that's what these letters are for, Jim—
    this timid prose that keeps
        trying on poetry's trendy clothes
           and dancing in front of a dirty mirror.

Not to make you into Ulysses. And not to make me into Kirk Douglas playing him in an old movie.

But to make sure
    you are remembered…

        and to make clear
           you are missed.

Before

The great use of life is to spend it
for something that will outlast it.

~ William James

The Collision

We knew "about" each other for a long time. But it took years and some amount of calamity for us to finally meet.

You'd been ordained, yet considered yourself an accidental deacon, in my dad's church—a church passing through the lower intestine of Southern Baptistismdomhoodness at the time.

The problem? My dad read books—biographies, novels, and other things along with the Bible—and he was known to call for calm, thoughtful consideration of theological disputes in committee meetings and other occasions of pious tumult. So, it goes without question that he was labeled a heretic by the convention.

And I... well... I was simply trying to recover from the funk of scrutiny and expectation that comes with having been a preacher's kid all my life.

But somewhere around our mid thirties, you were diagnosed with a rare form of cancer. Things changed. Okay... the Earth's axis shifted for you. Yet still, this was not the catalyst for our friendship.

A couple of years before, I'd gone through a divorce and was now doing my pitiful best to adapt to the amputated lifestyle of single fatherhood. And although I'd written songs since my teens and had already experimented with poetry, I began to feel the urge to *be* a writer.

Your health crisis caused a strikingly similar change in you right about the same time. And that's when—for some reason I cannot recall—we met for coffee at the Red Cup in Oklahoma City.

Sometimes the cosmos knows when it's time for two people
to collide, and so it makes the necessary arrangements, since
no one else will.

We needed each other…
    and the reason was simple…
        if not a bit worrisome—

we were both in the process
of coming out of the closet as…

                                    poets.

And here in the hubcap of the Great Plains, where politicians
hold an annual "Defunding of the Arts" gala and we bleed
Republican red at every football game and tent revival in every
county,
            this was no laughing matter.

That Trip to Ouray

Was I Right... or What?

We drove an hour or two out of the way on an already twelve-hour trek. I insisted that the chile rellenos at Doc Martin's in Taos really were worth the delay.

You doubted me for the entire stretch through Northwest Oklahoma and the top of the Texas Panhandle, right up to the moment when you took the first bite of the Anaheim green chile lightly fried in a pumpkin-seed, tortilla-chip crust and filled with goat cheese cream.

Granted, that bite came after one of their fabulous Horny Toad margaritas at a notably higher altitude than where we'd started out the day. But you seemed genuine enough in your gratitude for my persistence. And I'd say that after the second Horny Toad, you became downright effusive over your newfound love—for the rellenos, of course—to the point that we rhapsodized about all things Anaheim... and all things horny... all the way into the lemon-lime sunset and chile-powder clouds of Southern Colorado.

West by Northwest

Hindsight has me saying we barely survived the thin twisting wire of a rain-slicked Highway 550 between Durango and Ouray, especially with you—fresh out of the surgery that removed your right arm—behind the wheel and workin' the windshield wipers at the same time.

We had no idea this was the "Million Dollar Highway" that had killed more people than some of history's smaller wars.

Anyway, your old Mercury Cougar didn't have a mist or delay
function, and the wiper blades squealed like a bitter barfly in a
... on.
... we jiggled and wiggled our left-handed way up the barely
two lanes—with barely a stripe between them—and marveled
at the ornate portals of the southern Rockies.

And I can tell you now: it scared the hell out of me, friend.
But… like you wrote once, about the same trip… we were

> *heading west by northwest*
> *in search of poetry,*

and I knew you were needing to flesh out your concern
that the loss of your arm would not mean the end
of everything.

Brats & Beer

Since the workshop we'd signed up for didn't start 'til the next
morning, we threw bags in a wood cabin the size of a storage
shed—the best a couple of poets could afford—then headed
straight on down to Billy Goat Gruff's Biergarten for
bratwurst, sauerkraut, and some Red Stripe on tap.

We clinked glasses and centered our crosshairs on how much
we hated workshops, then went on to defend our attendance
at this one: we needed to get away… road trips stir the coals
of creativity… and, besides, the leader for this one is Stephen
Dunn—our favorite living poet writing in the English
language.

After last call at Gruff's, we walked the small stretch of Main
Street and landed in the Silver Eagle Saloon... for
and blunt talk about your job as a ... and
the shockingly creative ways human beings kill each other.

When the camera turned on me, I admitted I'd not been
sleeping much lately for talking all night to a beautiful new
problem in my life... a problem who wasn't mixing well with
the ex—at least not as well as the one who'd just left me...
the one I loved... and the one my little girl loved too.

And we never mentioned
   your medical bills...
   your life... your wife...
   the kids or the cancer,

because what you needed most at the moment was a break
from the statistical improbability of your future. You needed
brats, imported beer, and some clear evidence that my world
was going to hell too.

Over Enchiladas

We'd traveled a long, dangerous road and stretched a couple
of paper-thin budgets to spend all of two and a half days in
this in-depth workshop with Professor Dunn. (Just the
memory of it has me reediting the first paragraph of this piece
and cracking my knuckles in preparation for a big rework of
the last one. I'll need to hammer on it some fifteen to fifty
times before his spirit will rest.)

But the truer story began midstride the first session of the day
when we learned—along with some excellent tips, tools, and

poetic devices—that the good professor now lived in the throes of Parkinson's. Muscles and nerves expressed their minor confusion in his hands... hands we'd respected for years with an adoration like that of acolytes in the wings of the nave... hands we hoped would continue to deliver some of the best work we've ever read.

And so, maybe it was natural that when he saw my recently amputated heart there next to your recently amputated arm, he felt more comfortable standing next to us in the off hours.

Whatever the equation, that was how we found ourselves across the table from him that night with Coronas and cheese enchiladas smothered in red and green chile sauce. Through lunges of laughter and a few hysterical tears, we relaxed under the veil of entropy—our cells in unavoidable decline—and for a brief moment, filled with limes and salt, death lost an inch of ground... a finger's-worth of its grip.

The beer went down like Gilead's balm. The red sauce burned low and warm. And I learned more about poetry in the three courses of that one meal than a PhD—with all its courses combined—drummed up in five excruciating years.

The Hand You're Dealt

You splayed out the words on the table

    "prognosis"
      "radiation"
        "chemotherapy"

like frayed cards on green felt—a weak three-of-a-kind against the sarcoma's full house—as we talked about numbers and odds on this second round...

    and how your family... your poems—
      your hearts and diamonds—

now serve as inlay on the clubs and spades we'll wield in the gamble on this brutal, cellular poker match. And in a weak play for a little relief I reminded you of the fifty bucks I bluffed my way into with a pair of twos that one night a few years ago.

And we both...
          almost smiled.

Cowboys & Eskimos

Under the guise of researching an article on coffee shops for the *Oklahoma Gazette*, we sped north out of the city in your car, because mine had broken down and been towed back to Norman. But really, we were both just dyin' to get outta town—both dyin', deep inside, of very different damned things.

We eased into Stillwater, where you'd gone to school at OK State, under the solid black quilt that still covers the sky at night when you get far enough away from the dull glow of urban sprawl. And we couldn't smell the cattle yards over on the west end this time... figured the wind must have been from the south. But when the wind changes here, wayfarin' city-folk can get quite a good dose of the Great Plains' own form of tear-gas.

After a negligible amount of journalism, we popped into Eskimo Joe's, a famous jumpin' little juke joint where you'd spent a good bit of almost every night for four years of an education you can barely remember. And the cheap beer and cheese fries at this place were—no doubt—part of the reason for that.

Over a bowl of nuts at the bar I got an earful of wild stories about old times that weren't all good. One frat guy had punched a girl in the stomach over some microscopic disagreement. Another local with an unnaturally long, stretchy penis used to whip it out when drunk and do things with it I just don't wanna go into here—a guy named Slinky no less.

We each had a Boulevard Wheat or two on tap and a Little Joe burger with cheese. And you told me more sordid tales. And it had been a while since I'd had such a good time... since I'd breathed clean air above the clouds of failure that

had stalled out in my chest. And it seemed to do something of
the same for you.

So, we lingered as long as we could before we stepped back
out onto Elm Street. And you drove us all the way home—
with one arm and a slight beer buzz—down the dark thread
of I-35

with only the pale ale light
of a quarter-moon
and a good new
memory.

Have You Heard?

A daily glass of wine now kills women—science just told us
on late afternoon television. Something to do with its latest
empirical study. Of course, the research enlists a fifty percent
increase in breast cancer to warrant this grave statistic.

Just a week ago, according to other studies, that same glass of
wine helped them live longer because of all the antioxidants,
especially in the red stuff like Malbec and Merlot.

Anyway, since a new study revealing how that same glass of
wine now kills men too has not been released this week...

I'd like to offer this toast:

    Nothing, dear friend,
      is killing us faster
        than the news
          of all this.

Hoisting the Sails at Agora

Circumstances sometimes drive us down I-45 to Houston.
You, because of M.D. Anderson. Me, because of a prospect in
love who teaches English at Episcopal High School. But while
here, we'll take any chance we get to steal away to this Greek
coffeehouse and write at a small marble-top table by a second-
story window that overlooks the incessant traffic on
Westheimer.

Agora—where the gods are old and cranky, soccer goals on
TV make the rafters shake, and the jukebox cranks out either
Sinatra or something that sounds like bad Croatian pop.

You love the ship-like creaking in these driftwood stairs and
splintered floors. I love the ancient smell of myths and heroes.

Yes… there is something of the sea in this place—a floating
colony of lost souls left behind in the foamy wake of one of
Odysseus's unrecorded journeys.

And there is something of the port in this place as well—the
docks and pubs where you, my good friend, gather up
supplies and pack salt-encrusted bags for the big journey
across that last, dark ocean.

Trucks and Monsters

The news comes like a hydroplaning 18-wheeler in the rear-
view mirror. The cancer's back for the fourth time. And now
it's in the lungs and liver—the two worst places, we hear, it
can dig in its rotting yellow claws.

> But this time you won't be
> a young Beowulf, unarmed,
> tearing that huge scaly limb
> from Grendel's body. No...
>
> this time, my friend, you will be
> the old king battling the dragon
> with questionable equipment
> and substantial lower-back pain.

So, I look away from the mirror before impact... before the
mangle of trucks and ice... the clash of swords and monsters.

> So many dangers
> for so many centuries.
> So many ways to die.

Unaccustomed

At a reading in Wichita, Kansas, they'd arranged for us to
have separate top-floor suites in a nice new Hilton. They'd
even left baskets of chocolates, lint-rollers, and Perrier on the
wet bars in our sparkly, perfumed rooms.

It was too late to explain that, when it comes to poets, this
just isn't done. They were thinking of musicians. And fairly
successful ones at that.

Anyway, we forgave the faux pas and enjoyed the polished
tiles in clean showers that actually drained—along with the
popcorn and coffee in the kitchenettes—in spite of our
philistine selves.

But alone in my room that night, when I pulled back the soft,
spotless sheets and climbed in among the five or six white
feather pillows, I saw ol' Bukowski's ghost curled up in a fit of
laughter on the ersatz Italian sofa, flippin' through the
channels on the satellite.

And if ghosts do this sort of thing, I'd swear he raised a cheap
can of beer and grinned a toothy smart-ass toast with a big
ugly finger pointin' right at me:

   Don't get used to it, friend…

Note to Another Oklahoma Hitchhiker
(a response to Jim's poem, "Note to an Oklahoma Hitchhiker")

On the shoulder of I-35 South, just below Kansas, we spotted him with a thumb out at mile marker 218. The head and sideburns looked like a bad sequel to Elvis, especially with the big gold sunglasses to boot. The gut was a good match too, if maybe the King had lived on to eat a few more skillet-fried PBH n' banana sandwiches.

But none of that was enough to overshadow the bright pink sweatshirt and thin gray tights—tights that weren't workin' too hard to hide the main problem bulging down there in the southern plains. And to anchor the ensemble, he sported a spit-shined pair of foot-tall, black-leather army boots with neon-red laces all the way to the top.

With you doubled up in heaving laughter, I shook my head in amazement—as well as a certain amount of fear, to be honest—to the point that I wanted to pull over, but only to explain:

Look friend... some God-fearin'-bronc-bustin' Oklahoma cowboy is gonna screech to a stop on the shoulder—and very soon, I might add—grab the 12-guage shotgun from the rack in his back winder, jump out, and put   you   down.

And he's gonna do it believin' it's for your own good sake, as well as God's n' ever'body else's.

Multiplying Cells

She's twelve.
But she knows.

We coast down
May Avenue in OKC

on a frozen January Sunday
when she finally asks about it:

So how long does Jim have, Dad?

Well… that's a tough one Honey,
I answer… but then get pensive.

He's the best friend I have on the home front,
and she's in love with his rock star son.

I work out a quiet, well controlled,
Six months to a year, Punkin.

She reaches over…
grabs my hand…

holds it a long time.
And like I said…

She's twelve.
But she knows.

He Gave His Only

He left her in Santa Cruz.

He knew he had to do it…
    let her go.

It broke her heart.

But it left every organ in his withering body wrecked and
bleeding even worse than usual.

And so it was that a father—who has less than two semesters
according to his oncologists—drove off and left his daughter
at a small coastal college half a continent away… left her like a
sacrifice at the feet of bored gods who have always only
listened to our prayers when they felt like it.

And he bawls his yellow eyes out
while she blazes a new Pacific trail…

    the trail of her inchoate life
        that those bored bastard gods
            will not allow him to walk.

Human Subject Research

> *Today is the future*
> *if tomorrow never comes.*
>
> *Why not insist on*
> *a few interesting moments*
>
>   *every*
>   *day?*
>
>   —Jim Chastain
>   "Folding the Laundry"

You and LeAnn came over for a little party last night—some margaritas and cheese. Okay… quite a few margaritas and some cheese.

Tequila and beer are now your final, self-prescribed chemical cocktails in a long and gruesome series of failed chemotherapies. And though this new, self-conducted human subject research study has received no federal funding and is not expected to cure you, it has shown great results so far in your overall comfort level and relative enjoyment of the treatment sessions.

A nuzzling dog, our soft old couch, and the clinking glasses of good company provided a more relaxing atmosphere than the stale chairs, cold needles, and tubes of the cancer ward.

We offered neither grim prospects—while staring at a clipboard—nor false hope. We talked about poetry, music, and the kids' minor run-ins with the law. We laughed a lot… cranked the music…

and for just a little while,
there in the living room…

with all of us smiling
through a thin veil
of inebriation...

we forgot.

The Good Fight

Round 15, and you've fallen
back on the ropes, waiting
for the final upper-cut
that'll send you to the mat

where the doctors outside the ring
will slap the floor by your feet
and tell you not to get up this time.

> *Just stay down.*
> *We'll give you something*
> *for the pain.*

Your eyes—along with all
the eyes of your fans
weeping in the stands—
are red and swollen now,
most of the way to shut.

But, in the bloody end,
what's a boxer to do

whose only weapon
is a left hook?

Existential Solstice

This—the day that offers
the least amount of light—
rates as my favorite of the year...
this day and the hundred or so
that fall right before.

Nothing too philosophical about it,
except maybe that I smell more beauty
in the winter of things.

Spring tosses out dangerous promises
like rose petals at a white wedding.

But autumn's slow leak into December
teaches us to hold hands
as we come to grips with endings...

with where the inevitable swings
of the planet's axis are taking us.

After

A poet must leave traces of his passage, not proof.

~René Char

Ice and Snow

It came after a cold wet rain in the night that turned to sleet as the morning huddled under a gray blanket and coughed on the windows...

the call.

I poured coffee, schnapps, and my wrenching sadness into a chipped red mug and sipped for a long time at the table in the back room.

You had finally called the game—on account of heavy radiation—at 5:30 am on Christmas Eve...

      a touch of poetry,
      even in parting.

And now, an hour or so later, white ice is blowing sideways down the street as I listen to electronic sorrows and solace begin to pop up like corn into the inbox of my email.

Everybody remembers when they lost theirs, back when the Angel of Sarcoma ignored the blood above their doors as well. And I *Reply to All* my gratitudes... and I mean them. But this morning... we lost ours. A last breath among manger scenes and old black & white movies with Jimmy Stewart running through the soft wet snow of a second chance and Santa Claus convincing New York City, again, that he is indeed real.

And I know Jesus and Santa are always busy during this hectic season—because of overpopulation 'n all—but...

I'd really hoped too.

For You to Know

I woke up to the first white Christmas in a long time.

And now, in the sag of the afternoon, the wet sizzle and hiss of snow-logged logs in the fire purr behind the 24-hour marathon of *A Christmas Story* on TBS as flames flicker pink through the martini glass and bruised ice of a Cosmo shaken and poured by the grace of my lover's lime-licked fingers.

And I have lounged my way through worse holidays than this one, Jim—even here... today... in the shadow of your quiet, medicated death on yesterday's cold dawning—that last sunrise for which you'd lost the strength to get up and ponder.

Or maybe—after such a long December night—was it the most beautiful you ever rose to witness?

Dammit, friend. That is one iambic mystery I sure wish you could riddle me now. So much rides on resurrection versus hallucination, you know?

And I'm here, by the way, if you want to reach across. Though the angels may require that you wait until I'm really buzzed on some dark Tuesday night... some lost hour they're sure I'll forget. But if there is something... or someone... on the B-side of life, I know it's first gonna take them a good bit of their eternal time up there to convince you.

My Good Man
—written on the morning of… and for… your funeral

I toy with and twist around this block of absurdity in my
hands like a Rubik's Cube: over in North Korea, Kim Jong-il
lives on to threaten our species, while God… or chaos… or
some combination, asks you to step outside.

When the clearest truth is that there is no sense to be made of
such a malignant loss, those who remain must tie our shoes,
don our coats, then slip and drive on thin ice to the funeral.

❮ O ❯

You wanted no melodrama. No Auden telling us to

> *Stop all the clocks*
> *cut off the telephone,*

or Dickinson pining

> *How still the dancer lies.*

But, you asked me to say something. One last… cruel…
assignment in our ongoing game of words and poems.

And I know you're laughing over on the far shore of that
river, because—as it turns out—it can't be done.

So… as I stand here, reduced to the mediocrity of fact, I will
say, simply:

> *You have left a hole*
> *that no metaphor*
> *or clever word-play*
> *can fill.*

You have stumped the band.

And I appreciate this tough lesson
about art, love, and living.

And now…
   my good man…
      it is your turn.

At Your Funeral

They printed your poem in the funeral program without the title or the correct line breaks. But they got the words right. They were trying, I suppose, to get it all onto one page.

Maybe that's what funerals are for. The grief is too long, and we need, somehow, to gather it up into one place... some terminal and exhausted space. Besides, they did do a fairly good job of following your specific orders. Well... except that they held it in the church sanctuary, I'm afraid. Sorry about that. But, my friend, too many people loved you, and most of them showed up. The smaller room—the one you'd wanted—wasn't up to the gentle outpouring of muted sobs and stunted laughter.

But the stories from the pulpit were good, and they marked your desire for a touch of irreverence quite well. I could sense that God, in the robe and slippers of a Tuesday morning, was relaxed and having a much better time with your crazy, eclectic clan than the more acute company he's required to dress up for on Sundays.

And, as usual, I got no clear answers from him to the questions I had about you. I don't know why it would've been such a bother just to let me know that the angels had in fact greeted you with a tray of salt-rimmed margaritas and that you were, finally, able to hold two at once.

But I've learned over time to accept the silence he's compelled to honor and to walk with him in my own irascible way on the cold back highways he's led me down—

collar up...
            hands in pockets...
                        mouth mostly shut.

The Blessèd Bones

We talked a lot about daughters—those wonderful, blessèd
creatures granted to us by divine retribution for all the things
we thought about the daughters of other men when we were
younger and driven by the demands of natural selection.

And I remember how you'd gasp between fits of tears when
you thought about the cruel truth that you would not be the
one to walk yours down the aisle.

So, I thought it important to let you know, Jim...

yours sat on the front row of the funeral—straight in front of
me as I spoke. And in that sea of sorrow and support,

no one... no
one, my friend,
shed more tears
from the bones
of her eyes

than she.

Highs and Lows

And we talked a lot about art... movies and poetry in
particular... and how so much of it seemed to be little more
than the effluent of a mediocre liberal arts education.

High art, we thought, was a pedantic nose-bleed in a boring
museum. Mystified faces all aflush with academically assigned
admiration... heads tilting way back to keep all our confusion
from rushing out onto the marble floor.

Low art, we felt certain, was a roving Thomas Kinkade mobile
home art gallery—that and wedding toast poetry written by
fathers the night before as they sit in a drunken stupor, each
one crying over the cost of such a questionable match for his
little girl.

Good art was, of course, what we were doing.

The Only Thing Worse

We also talked some about dying...

> about how Christians were often the worst at
> helping you do it—quoting Romans 8:28 through
> little bursts of pitiful nervousness...

> and about how that one doctor might have been
> the only thing worse than the worst.

You were worried about your son, mid-stride his straggle-
haired teens—the two of you so close for so long. And I'm
worried about him too—the black-stone stare at your funeral
and the strange metabolic shock he's walking around in now.

You obsessed over the day when LeAnn—headed down some
other road—might remarry.

> Would she enjoy some straight conversation with
> a pleasant, less poetically-inclined someone?

> Would he bring the kids thoughtful... or lame...
> Christmas presents?

> Would she love a new life, some new address
> with him?

All these shards of plausibility slashed away at your already
disintegrating abdomen—the only thing worse than the
chemo.

Way to Go

That last afternoon we talked—there in the big soft chairs of your living room with Green Bay playin' some other team for some playoff—you told me you were now down to two horrible choices with your treatment but didn't have the energy for either one.

So, you turned to funeral plans. A few friends, a few stories— and keep 'em funny, dammit. You had asked my dad to officiate. You wanted no melodrama, and you thought he'd be good at controlling that. You also wanted me to speak at some point. But your main concern was... absolutely... *no* religious bullshit.

And then... you had written one last left-handed poem you wanted read at the very end of the ceremony. That's when a few tears attacked our eyes.

You switched off the TV. And after a minute or two of silence, we managed to laugh a little over some comment you made. A couple of guys in the Great Plains get uncomfortable with tears and silence, even in the face of death. But still, I left thinking we'd have at least three or four more times to talk about the details.

And now, days after your funeral, I just finished the last poem in John Ashbery's latest book, and it didn't make any more sense than the first one of his pieces I read years ago. He's eighty-one and still churnin' out hieroglyphs that only a small number of literary archeologists and wannabes claim to understand. And I'm happy for him to do it.

But friend... I've got your one last poem here in front of me this evening... and at forty-six, you made enough gut-wrenching sense to make up for everything Ashbery never said.

Revenance

Poetry soothed the savage
dissonance that radiated
through the empty halls
and chambers of your body.

Like the buzz, crackle,
and hum of a warped LP
twirling out an old accordion
behind a slick French crooner,

the needle in a poem's groove
had the ring of preservation
and gave you the chance
to intone notes of hope

and hear how they echo
in the bell of the horn...
ripples of remembrance
in your lingering love.

Mugs and Buckets

I thought about heaven today—
that place our more educated parts
mock in public, but in private, parts
(other parts) of us love to love the idea of...

some cloudy, white-bearded otherwhere
that saves the better parts of us
from the all-night keggers
of worms and maggots.

So when I heard this morning, someone tell the amazing story
of the London Beer Flood in 1814, I thought about you and
heaven.

Oh Jim, massive vats on the roof of a brewery at Tottenham
Court buckled under the fermented weight of a million and
more liters of porter... beer that broke through a 25-foot
brick wall and then raged its way through the parched streets
of St. Giles.

Londoners flooded the avenues with mugs and buckets...
pots and pans... some simply burying their heads in an open-
mouthed baptism of hops and barley.

Anyway, I thought about you and heaven today.

Great Plans

You've got me thinking about arrangements... some amount of instruction for loved ones when it comes to my eventual demise. I've done this before at the expense of good paper.

In some poem in some book, I once laid out an elaborate plan as to where to spread my ashes... something egomaniacal enough to require airplanes, helicopters, and four separate locations. And I ended it with a clever quip about wanting to be "hard to find."

You chose the route of ashes too... told me you were sick and tired of the strange mushroom your body was morphing into—a battered ship's hull taking on a sad, polluted sea. And I'll be blunt—that earlier photograph of you, down in front of the pulpit at the funeral service, did look a bit better.

But, back to some plan for my encroaching end. Hmm... I'm not sure yet... but here's one that's growing on me:

how about a massive funeral pyre out on some parched and distant stretch of the Great Plains—that infinite grassy shoreline of my Viking odyssey. You know... like an open casket version of cremation.

Too Late Sherlock

Man, you would have let Robert Downey, Jr. have it in one of
your scathing movie reviews. But I loved him as Sherlock
Holmes in the recent updated version that hit theaters for the
holidays.

He seems screwed up enough to play Sir Doyle's red-eyed-
maniac of a messed up protagonist. And every time his neck
twitched as he plucked the dull gut-strings of that warped and
musty violin—out in the periphery of his catatonic gaze—I
saw how you have me locked up in the throes of deductive
reasoning lately… hunting for little clues… signs of
malpractice.

Was there anything about the type of mud on your Italian
leather shoes… or the chemicals they kept cooking up for you
in Moriarty's fluorescent and bubbling pharmacy… or the
timing of the doctor's choice to cut off your writing arm?

Was there anything about the books of poems you were
reading… or the ones you were typing with the forefinger of
the hand that was left…

      something so elementary…

        I might have been able
                   to save you?

Who's in Charge Here?

I've lowered my eyes, and my standards, down to Bukowski
again—the original dirty old man of American letters.

He cuts no slack in any line—not even the fine one between
life and death—like the opening phrase he shoved out the
window of this morning's reading time...

there is nothing subtle about dying or
dumping garbage.

As a literary wrecking ball, who cared more than he gets credit
for, he reminds me—with an inebriated push to the back—
that I have yet to raise a fist and middle finger to the gods and
angels assigned to your case. I see clear and cosmic signs of
celestial malpractice. (And I won't mention the names of
strung out and psychotic celebrities in the news lately who
heaven allows to live on.)

And man... I'm thinkin' that if even the deities and
principalities in charge of poets and writers are now just drunk
and pukin' in some alley behind a bar because they're sick of
their thankless work and immortality,

we're all fucked.

Going over "Details"

When the cancer came back again, to shake you like a sock in
its drooling mouth, the good professor Dunn sent you... as a
quiet consolation... an unpublished poem he'd written about
his brother—knowing, as a sage poet might, that to say
anything more would sound like an awkward moment at a
high school reunion.

You treasured it. And we agreed he'd nailed it in these lines:

> *My brother is talking about his ice-maker*
> *because a man can't talk about his lymphoma*
> *and chemo every minute of the day.*

That said so much for us. Because I stunk at discussing cancer
with you. And you were glad of it.

I thought you must be as tired of it as anyone—a concern I
had that I stirred into my selfishness to try and hide it.
Besides... we had poems and pink cocktails to ponder—their
fashion and effect, as well as their relative impact on our sense
of manhood.

So here's to it, my friend...

> to all things pink
>   and poetic...

and to this broken brotherhood
that staggers on beyond death.

Word for Word

I do it on days when more fruitful citizens go to work in suits
and do more productive stuff for the world...

those days when I throw guitars and books into the Camry
and drive... say... south... to say... maybe Austin and sit in
some coffee shop and watch those more useful people get on
elevators while I wait for happy hour to start at Manuel's
across Congress Avenue, because I know a couple of those
four-dollar margaritas are gonna help me deal with my general
feelings of loss and nonproductive uselessness to a society
that's scared of poems and songs about love and politics...
but especially death.

           And...   ok...

now I'm across the street sipping on said margarita, trying like
hell to remember what it was you said the last time we talked
while you curled up in a blue robe in your easy chair with a
box of apple juice—the only thing you could keep down
anymore.

And I can't remember it word for word, but it had something
to do with your belief that this...   these poems...
these songs...   do matter,
and that I shouldn't
give up.

Heavy Weights

Just a few days before you, one of the only youth ministers I ever liked—who worked at one of the only churches I'm still able to step inside without feeling I might have eaten some bad mayonnaise the night before—died of a mysterious cocktail that involved a barbell and cardiac arrest.

And I really liked him, Jim. And the two of you together brought a lot of death for the holidays… darker shades of blue here in this holy season that already bruises so easily.

But both of you understand, I'm sure, that I'll soon have to turn my attention back to the living. A beautiful wife-to-be breathes by the fire in the living room down the hall. She requires little… but deserves much more. And money doesn't grow on poetry.

Then there's the pubescent minefield of a thirteen-year-old daughter. Both of you knew plenty about that gorgeous pain. And, David, you survived it three times as a single dad. So… I can't believe you lived as long as you did.

Maybe I've lost my grip on the delicate protocol of the passing of friends, but I can't bring myself to talk to you any differently now than I would have if you'd done me the favor of sticking around.

But know that I paid close attention to Bukowski when he told me, on page 21 of *The Roominghouse Madrigals*:

> it's not
> the history
> of countries
> but the lives of men.

And you two burned hot amidst the cool of the 21st Century's zoned-out mediocrity—this wasteland of smart phones, bubblegum, and reality television. You were heavy weights on the battered scales of what matters in this world.

Nip and Tuck

Now, only a half-year removed from our last adventure, I already squint and cock my head in the act of recalling our stories... stories of bare-chested beer-bellied bubbas, hitchhiking Elvises, and the bombs of humanity that exploded all around us on street corners, on-ramps, and dim stages where poets and writers tanked at major readings or in the wasteland of Open-Mic Night.

I've buffed out so many scratches and dings in the paint of our stories, I now worry about their cosmetic integrity.

At the same time, "the truth" has always felt like salty taffy in my mouth—the way it yanks on loose teeth and takes forever to digest. And "the facts" of any matter seldom make people lean forward in their cushiony seats... seats on the front rows of lives that are filled enough already with the hassle and boredom of "what actually happened."

So, since you're not here to check up on me anymore, I'll go ahead with my mostly non-fiction version of the way things went.

Belly Up

It's a medical condition they tell me I aggravate with coffee
and chocolate. So I'm writing you this morning, of course,
with a nice hot cup of Columbian dark roast and one of
Dodee's brownies—the ones you loved so much.

And I always popped my neck and knuckles when we would
salt up rims and pour tequila and sweet liqueur into lime juice,
when we both knew the cancer had now laid hands on your
liver as well as your lungs.

What was I supposed to do? What were you supposed to do,
for that matter? You had a cocktail of acid fire and Mexican
love that you lived to light up and throw through the windows
of your dilapidated body.

Could we have saved you there at what we knew was the end?
Should we have slit the throat of that joy and drained it dry on
the bloodstained altar of slightly better health?

I don't know…

I don't know any damn thing about your untenable death
anymore.

But tonight I know I'll raise

      in your honor…

the one
          that's probably
                killing me too.

The Low-Down

My soon-to-be-wife—since I can't bring myself to say *fiancée* yet—popped over to your house while I was out of town to spend some girl-time with your wife—since I can't bring myself to say *widow* yet.

And though reports vary, I don't at all doubt that decent amounts of wine and cheap vodka washed over their questions, humorous bafflements, and complaints—burgundy and silver streams dissolving the salt of a few tears, I'm sure.

That is... until the back-slap of ol' Bacchus nudged them over into the realm of outright laughter about the antics and inadequacies of their men... and others. These are the nights... the rites and rights of women that they so deserve... the nights and rites of their long-suffering that affirm the reputations we so rightly earned.

Anyway, I don't know what kind of view the windows offer you in the afterlife, but I'd appreciate any details or dirt you could slip me... maybe under some extra-dimensional door...

because little parties like this make me so damn nervous.

All the Same

In light of that last letter, I don't know how much you're
allowed to say from wherever it is you are, but the questions
float in every morning lately with the smell of the coffee
brewing.

Do the painters and poets
continue to starve in heaven,
because heaven knows
it keeps their work honest?

Do the singers and songwriters
sell no CDs up there either—
because some devious angel
wired the entire place for file-sharing—
so they have to wage their limping gospels
in loud bars and coffee shops to the few
who are inebriated or hurt enough
to need the sideways message?

Do the prophets still sit
ignored at the city gates
because they've never learned
how to dress properly
or speak in words
that people can understand?

Anyway… I'm only asking because I wouldn't want things to
be too unrecognizable up there.

The Way…
Things Go

Angels,
we have grown apart.

—Charles Bukowski

It's an old picture of my daughter,
around three or four, holding out
a river stone to the camera.

A sweetness to baffle
all reason and sense.

I've carried it in my wallet
for a decade… looked at it
from the losing end
of single-fatherhood
with a sad desperation.

Hands and photographs
weren't designed to hold
anywhere near as much
as we keep wishing they could.

And sometimes the good things
slip away, while the worst
remain inside us and grow—
dark clouds building
on an MRI's horizon.

So, when the surgeon cut off
the hand you used the most,
more and more slipped away
with every menacing month

until... finally...
the hand you had left
lost its grip on the angels
gathered around you... angels

who held on with theirs
as long as they could.

Man vs. Their Nature

After diapers and car seats… the rides to soccer practice and some school supplies… how much do they really need us, Jim?

Their childhoods tease us with a few diaphanous days—maybe even years. But then the sequence of numbers that end in 'teen' count down like a hormonal launch code for warheads that biology aims straight at parents… parents who, because of the strange chemistry of unconditional love, stand square in the path… eyes blinking in bewilderment. And the only protections that same lousy biology offers us? Denial and a decent amount of memory loss.

We accept nature's verdict like we would an orange jumpsuit on processing day in the penitentiary—slowly putting it on in that captive silence—and then we begin to serve our time.

And the angry warden of cell division gave you no special treatment either, as a parent with cancer and only one arm. It shut the iron doors on you, just like everybody else. Only… you died there in the slammer, just months before her 20s—the age when daughters sometimes release us early, for good behavior.

Walking Shadows

Sometimes I lose it... like a wallet in a movie theater...

what it was we thought we were doing—a couple of poor players—with our poetry in those last few years between your ambiguously helpful surgeries and my small, spectacular stream of disintegrating relationships.

But some artistic, if not delusional, force kept pushing us out onto the road, in spite of our physical and mental journeys of the damned.

And, looking back, I do wish our quixotic travels could have had a few more windmills and castles on the set... some cinematic splashes here and there along the lines and bends of Route 66—one of our favorite trails when we could swing it.

And I'd've liked an ending more like Butch and Sundance— revolvers firing and flashing as we strut and fret our way out into a certain, yet glorious death.

But the disease forced you to follow the script, even though none of the actors in the screenplay liked it.

So, we played our parts... planted our poems like literary landmines in the red dirt and brimstone of the Southwest... until... your hour upon the stage was up.

Back Here...

Back here...
>we still fight with the people we love the most, even though we've tried to tear down the heavy curtains that cover the filmy windows of our hearts. Always grasping for more truth and light. Truth that seldom makes us kinder or easier to deal with. Light that Goethe begged for right up to his end.

Back here...
>we still gorge ourselves on 16 oz. black angus burgers and shove the dead fat of fries straight into our arteries while others shrink to bones in the deserts of countries our high school geography teachers failed to mention.

Back here...
>we still throw young soldiers and smart bombs at dumb wars for reasons we can't quite put a political finger on.

Back here...
>the followers of Christ still refuse to believe their history was painted with the same blood and written in the same dark ink that the followers of one interpretation of Muhammad apply with strap-on brushes today.

Back here...
>we still clamor for an answer
>>we'll never get
>to a question
>>>>we cannot frame...

a question
>>>>and answer
that you
>>>>now possess.

In the Cards

For that first 35 years, we played the game of LIFE, took the "START COLLEGE" route, and stopped at the mandatory "JOB SEARCH" space.

The game doesn't have CAREER CARDS for lawyer or professor. So we settled for ACCOUNTANT and TEACHER… though we'd both secretly hoped for the ARTIST CARD, in spite of how it would guarantee we'd get stuck with the lowest SALARY CARD and only be able to afford the SPLIT-LEVEL house from Faultline Real Estate.

Oh well… we accepted our stations, spun the wheel, and advanced the correct number of spaces—made that required STOP at the WEDDING CHAPEL. Kids came along with the HOUSE DEEDS, STOCKS, and HOMEOWNER'S INSURANCE, as well as quite a few fees, penalties, and hidden taxes… until…

you discovered that lump on your right triceps. Suddenly you were thrown out of the world of Milton Bradley and into the land of Parker Brothers, sliding back and forth in the game of SORRY! You had a whole new set of cards to learn—moving forward 10… or back 1. The 7 CARD allowed you to split moves between two pawns, but there were so many decisions to make, forms to fill out, numbers to go over.

Once or twice, with the help of doctors, you pulled the 2 CARD that allowed you to DRAW AGAIN. But there were so many 4's that required you to move backward. And, in the end, we just couldn't get all your pieces into the SAFETY ZONE—a little breathing room so you could get them all HOME. Every time you'd round a corner, the sarcoma would knock one of your organs back to START. Yet… you spun the wheel and drew the cards much longer than the specialists thought you would. And you did it with an amazing amount of poetry and poise.

I'd Push the Buttons

I deleted your number,
    finally,
        out of my phone.

For months I'd push the buttons
    leading up to removal, but never could
        punch that last one to finish the job.

The cancer stole your body,
    then… right at the very end…
        your mind on Christmas Eve.

And I just haven't been able
    to bring myself to do it
        until now.

The First September Without

like my father's come to pass
seven years have gone so fast
wake me up when September ends

While sipping coffee back in a dark corner at the Sleeping Dog Tavern in Santa Fe, your favorite Green Day song sprang from the stereo system like a skittish horse early out of the starting gate.

I shuddered a bit and spilled a few brown drops on the pages of my journal. Then a few tears broke loose from my sideswiped eyes as I did my best not to make an unfashionable scene in front of the bartender and waitress.

So, with my hands gripping the reigns of my flailing eyebrows, I tried to keep my feet in the stirrups and my focus on the track lane dead ahead...

while preparing myself for the inevitability of the fall.

seven years have gone so fast
wake me up when September ends

The Lost Suppers

No poems can please for long or live
that are written by water drinkers.

~Horace

Bread Among Brothers

A good number of the good Southern Baptists we grew up
with will see your last supper poem, and especially my
gluttonous adventure with it, as nothing more than an insult
to Jesus and the da Vinci-enhanced vision of that evening he
spent with his disciples at the table.

Some of them will see this
because they are glancing
at poetry... not reading it.

Some will see it because they've made it their mission in life to
spot insults to Jesus and point them out, religiously, to poor
souls who are not paying enough attention to things. After all,
without them, God himself might lose track of some of the
more noteworthy lapses in moral rectitude.

Others will believe it because believing otherwise would force
them to stare square into the eyes of death and the pain of
premature, if not indefensible, loss.

But neither of us intended any disrespect to this story—one
of the many great ones that raised us.

We simply see Jesus,
more than ever,
as a beautiful example
of what anyone would want
there at the end of things...

     dinner with friends.

The Last Supper

by Jim Chastain (11-23-08)

The menu's not that difficult,
a smorgasbord of favorite dishes
from trusted restaurants.

Appetizers would include
fried mushrooms from Hideaway,
cheese fries from Eskimo Joe's,
lettuce wraps from P.F. Chang's,
chips and salsa from Border Crossing,
resurrected somehow just for me,
LeAnn's broccoli mushroom dip,
and my own guacamole.

For soups and salads I'd order
hot and sour soup from Lido,
La Madeleine's tomato basil soup,
my Dad's hot chili,
and dinner salads from Victoria's.
That's it.

The main course would be a brunch,
because I do love a good breakfast.
Omelets from Jimmy's Egg,
waffles from Original Pancake House,
The Blue Dome Diner's French toast,
lasagna rolls from Victoria's,
butternut squash ravioli from Olives,
barbecue from Dink's,
mango chicken from Misal,
grilled salmon from Cheever's,
a Nirvana Roll from In the Raw,
dutch oven potatoes from Iron Starr,
Kathy's homemade potato salad,

cheese bread from Pepperoni Grill,
my great grandmother's green beans
and her apple butter to smear
on bread from the County Line.

For drinks and desserts, I'd serve
cinnamon rolls from Aspen Coffee,
lattes from Shades of Brown,
cherry Danishes from La Baguette,
strawberry banana cake from Leo's,
Rusty's Crimson and Crème custard,
my mom's pecan pie,
along with swirls from La Luna,
and Cheshiritas.

No, the menu would be easy.
The difficult decision would be
whom I should invite
to sit down at the table.

The Poem that Launched a Million Calories

This was no "last meal" request—a modest table set with a
few courses of favorites, like a popcorn bowl full of Captain
Crunch and four orders of super-sized fries. You wrote a
voluminous poem that you revised, edited, but mostly added
to, while leaves fell all over the last autumn that would allow
you to really enjoy your mother's pecan pie.

No, this was a lengthy and lustful list... from the six
appetizers, and four different soups and salads... to the
fifteen main courses, three drinks involving caffeine or tequila,
and five artery-pounding desserts. An amazing amount of
food, even for a man who no longer needed to watch his
weight.

As it turns out, though, the cancer robbed your palate's
passion, as well as your stomach's will to hold it, before you
could get around to fulfilling this epic and final *tour du
gastronome*.

And now... in the summer after the winter that stole you...
how ridiculous it is—even selfish, considering my profane
love for fried food and multicolored drinks—to entertain the
idea that tackling the list myself... checking off each victual...
plate for plate, bowl for bowl...

would somehow
honor you.

The Sacrifice

Before I embark on this odyssey of sodium, saturated fat, and
processed sugar—please consider a few concerns on my part.

To begin with... I worry about my blood pressure and beltline. You had some downright extravagant caloric proclivities,
my friend. And I already fight the "whole new wardrobe"
battle every damn day of my damn life... an initial problem
that plays heavily into the next.... which would be...

How'm I gonna pay for all this, man? Not only do I have to
buy the meals, you've got me running all over Northeast
Oklahoma, then down to the underwear-soakin' humidity of
Houston and back through Dallas on the way to the hellacious
heat of Las Vegas... and I mean the Nevada one.

But all that pales before the marching orders that underlie the
chief concern of your poem... something you mentioned at
the very end...

> "whom I should invite
> to sit down at the table."

So now I have to bring along family and friends as well?

The Power of Velveeta

chips and salsa from Border Crossing,
resurrected somehow just for me

All you'd wanted were the chips and salsa.
Such a small request. Such an impossible task...

since they'd closed the place down not long before you wrote
your poem.

For decades though, Border Crossing was an institution in our
little town. Loved loyally by the locals who loved it, it was a
wonderful taste of Northern New Mexico in a state that owes
too much of its limited understanding of Mexican food to the
heavy, colonizing hand of the over-sized state below us with
its penchant for sour cream and Velveeta. They allowed none
of that at Border Crossing... where the beans were left
whole... not even fried the first time.

Just recently, their salsa and blue corn enchilada recipes did
resurrect for a brief time in a little two-story joint on Campus
Corner, when two cooks from the Crossing opened up a place
called Justin's. But it closed down too... to make way for
some place that has something to do with sushi and jazz and
someone's idea that college students would be into such a
trendy combo.

And I don't know what it means to say that even resurrection
can fail. But... the thought makes me hurt all over again... for
you.

Why I Lick the Bowl

La Madeleine's tomato basil soup

I taste something of the holy blood
in this red potion...

    something of the tomato's sacrifice
    where the basil hints of scars...

    something of the salt of the earth—
        probably a good 1,000mg of it—
    and the way it preserves us...

    and something of the baptismal waters
    in its sacred broth that sustains life.

And I worried about this dish because I know Pablo Neruda
would have done a much better job of immortalizing this red
fruit that—let's be honest—tastes suspiciously like a
vegetable.

But I see something of Jerusalem's Upper Room in the dark
wood and heavy stone of La Madeleine... some subtle touch
of da Vinci's divine vision.

And this vermilion soup, that inspires such spiritual devotion
among its disciples, really is that good...

    especially since they thicken it...

        with corn starch and crack.

Midnight in the Garden

lettuce wraps from P.F. Chang's

I went with the tofu version over the standard chicken, Jim.
But, understand… I was with a beautiful woman who's a
vegetarian because of the mind-bendingly egregious practices
of factory farming—a cause for deep distress and concern in
her sensitive soul. However, before I put the blame on her, I
have to be honest and tell you that I've seen much of the
evidence for myself, and I'm just sayin'…

Ahh… but I doubt you're worried much about this kind of
thing anymore. So let me get back to what matters in the
equation:
> The woman is beautiful
> and has a sensitive soul…

the one whom I invited "to sit down at the table" and share
my half carafe of white zin.

And your deep concern for the sake of those closest to you
was the blood-sweat on the forehead of your poems and our
road-talks in those last years… a concern, by the way, our
waiter did not offer us today with the shocking intrusion of
his thick, sharply-upturned, heavily-waxed, brown handlebar
moustache. Wowzers… that thing was a specimen.

But I know that loved ones mattered… terribly… to you. And
I was with you on some of those occasions when you got
down on your knees and wept in your own Gethsemane over
the good and grieving hearts you'd be leaving behind.

And I tried to be a good disciple and sit with you in that
garden.

A Bottle Among Friends

I lit a candle on the dark wood desk in the Poet's Room at
Blue Rock. It flickered in front of a sea-green bottle—

STERLING
VINEYARDS

1997

NAPA VALLEY
M E R L O T

The bottle stands before a window that frames a black and
green copse of wet cedar and rock… cedar and rock wet from
last night's Maelstrom of lightning and rain… cedar and rock
now resting amidst a haphazard karaoke choir of drunk and
weeping cicadas.

And the label on the bottle bears a handwritten note at the
top—a memento for the end of one of the toughest, most
tedious and interminable trials of my life—

The Toast at Blue Rock
celebrating Nathan's PhD…

And these are the friends who saw me through it.
And this has my mind continuing its work on your puzzle—

whom I should invite
to sit down at the table.

A puzzle I now believe I should carefully continue working
on… piece by piece… for the rest of my days.

Family Fortune

hot and sour soup from Lido

Here in the throes of no particular afternoon, the only other customers were a much older and odder couple that seemed to be enjoying no particular date. And while any movement of the neck or back looked like it hurt, something of a quiet contentment slow-danced in their eyes and occasional smiles.

Maybe the money they'd put back survived the tanked economy somehow, and they were out throwin' it around so the grandkids won't have to fight over it.

> The principle business of life is to enjoy it.
>
> —Her fortune cookie...

Maybe they never trusted the economy and stashed away hundred dollar bills for half a hundred years in a fire-box under the tool cabinet in the back of the shed where no conniving son could ever find it.

Whatever the story, quite a little feast sprawled out over the table in front of them, and they appeared quite happy to be there... alone... together.

> The happiest circumstances are close to home.
>
> —My fortune cookie...

I couldn't tell if hot and sour soup was among the many items in their extravagant spread, but a big bowl of it steamed between my love and me.

And the heat and spicy bite of it
burned and bathed me
with something of the abiding love
I believe they must hold for each other.

Deep-Fried Tradition

fried mushrooms from Hideaway

I got a chintzy stem of cheap white zin to go with them.

I know… I know. It should've been a big ol' draught of beer.
But man, I'm sacrificing so much for this pilgrimage as it is—
my arteries… my omentum. So please.

On the dipping sauces, I went with creamy Italian and
marinara because the waitress felt that the ranch overpowers
the spices and delicate flavor of the batter they fry the buttony
little shrooms in.

Well, I have to say… there was nothing delicate about the
flavor, and I never tasted any spices… unless… deep-fried-to-
a-crisp is a spice… which in Oklahoma, I suppose, just might
be the greasy case.

But don't take this to mean I didn't like them. Anything
dipped in enough tradition, peanut oil, and creamy sauce is
going to rate in my book. And this pizza joint, here in this
little cow town where you got your degree between all the
wild frat-driven nights of bacchanalia…

           just has somethin' special all over it.

Bursting My Bubbles

cinnamon rolls from Aspen Coffee

Okay… so we both agreed they put crystal meth in the
frosting of these messy babies. So, what's not to like? And I
went ahead and ordered one of their lattes too, because you
loved the beautiful leaf-like foam-art they always perform on
top.

And, by the way, the girl on the machine today was definitely
on her game.

But the longer I stared at the labyrinthine pattern of bubbles
in the brown and white striations of foam, the more I felt a
burn in the memory that the last time I'd admired it… had
been with you. We'd read at some gig you got us over by the
campus, that all of three people attended, but you didn't care
because you couldn't wait to show me this place.

So…
as I sit here alone… now…
on 7th Avenue in Stillwater, Oklahoma…
pecking away at what I love most in life—

      taking a hit of caffeine, along with some flour and sugar
      (and crank-laced frosting), while I write in a coffee shop—

I can't deny that some sacred amount
of the cinnamon soul in this place
has been lost
forever.

Baking Time

cherry Danishes from La Baguette

A generous and luscious bit
   of butter and love
      must go into these.

And when they throw in the sugar and three-hundred-
something degree heat, it's all gonna work some kind of
crystal magic on the cherries and cream cheese.

The best things in life—from pastries to wine... from coffee
shops to human beings—must break down in the throes of
some organic and elementally ordained process before they
find their purpose.

The great sadness comes, of course, when things are left in
the oven too long—like you... with the chemo and
unrelenting radiation—

the cure being
   what ultimately
      killed you.

Dr. Sushi in Nirvanaland

a Nirvana Roll from In the Raw

O sushi roll topped
    with teriyake-ish eel...
sesame seeds and scallions...
    before thee I kneel.

I sing the praises of
    your crab cake and jalapeño...
your avocado, cream cheese,
    and tuna rolled in masago.

And I'd die for a drop, a shot...
    anything'd be fine.
Even a smudgy tumbler
    or 2-liter beer stein

of that creamy habanero
    sauce that they drizzle
over your goodness
    and rich sushi sizzle.   Yes...

I would merrily drink it
    or suck it through a straw.
I would lap it like a dog
    off the table at In the Raw.

On pancakes or cookies...
    even Turkey Spam.
But especially on
    green eggs and ham.

Not That I'm Old

The Nirvana Roll did deliver on its name last night, Jim. And the outdoor patio in the back was so breezy and romantic— Christmas lights zigzagging overhead between the oaks and Chinese elms. Even the air covered us like a chenille blanket and threatened no extreme of temperature.

I would have changed only one thing…

the horrific background music playing plenty too loudly on the waterproof speakers.

They pulsed a steady stream of whatever it is that the retail industry thinks the 20-something crowd wants—a style that haphazardly combines all the worst elements of hip-hop, rap, and pop into one odious and insufferable genre filled with lyrics clearly indicative of this generation's addiction to Internet porn.

True. I'm 45.

But consider a small recent purchase made by my wife-to-be—my wife-to-be who is much younger. (Save your comments.)

One late afternoon, after a James McMurtry concert downtown, she brought home a little round pin-on button that boldly proclaims:

IT'S NOT
THAT I'M OLD

YOUR MUSIC
REALLY DOES
SUCK

Having Eggs and Options

Omelets from Jimmy's Egg

Mid-morning in mid-America on no particular Monday, we pretty much had the place to ourselves… except for three ladies in pink and purple scrubs who chose the table right behind me for some reason—over the 40 to 50 other options. They seemed pleasant enough though, at first.

We ordered the veggie omelet, since your list did not specify. And we shared it, since this gastronomic quest you've sent me on is raising the bad numbers on the charts of all my major health indicators.

This four-egg fluffy yellow beast was the size of a loaf of bread. Okay… maybe a small loaf. But still… it came with a greasy pile of hashbrowns almost as big, and a basket with two slices of their dark brown raisin toast, each one the size of a 19th century British novel. Okay… maybe more like a 21st century rerelease paperback.

Anyway… as I griped about the sodium and cholesterol to my accomplice, the ladies behind us began to speak in animated tones about some test they'd taken yesterday. Words like surgery, drugs, prosthetics, and cancer stung the back of my neck like I'd backed into a droning hive of well-armed memories.

And I realized, in a sudden squall of guilt, that you would've given anything to still be here…

dying slowly from fat and calories
instead of so quickly
from the cancer.

B.M.S.

*They are strange but simple folk who sing hallucinated by
a brilliant point of light trembling on the horizon.*

—Federico García Lorca, "Deep Song"

Lately, when the car drags into Austin, we've been sharing the
table with a small, beautifully disgruntled cadre of artists and
thugs. And they have me thinking on how, towards the end,
you had little patience for sharing the table with anyone
except the carefully chosen. Some folks, bless their hearts,
never were going to get what it was you did, and did *not*, need
to hear anymore.

That's why you would've loved this group, Jim. And they
would've loved you. They're comfortable with all the nuances
of temporality and terminality. They slap death in the face
every day, in some way or another.

We call our gatherings the Brunch for Misanthropes Society...
even if we're drinkin' whiskey at midnight or margaritas in the
morning.

These are the Ishmaels and Rahabs—the darker brothers and
sisters—who burn at the distant end of the candle... the
dangerous end of the horizon.

These are the disfigured prophets who make Job look like a
juvenile gypsy who has yet to earn his soul-stripes.

These are the friends who ignore your calls when the song...

      the painting... the student... or the story...

breaks water...
              and begs to breathe.

Fools and Messes

Rusty's Crimson and Crème custard

No one else in Rusty's this afternoon was likely giving much thought to the history of custard… this eggy gift from the Middle Ages.

What a snoot. And what an arrogant assumption for me to make.

But, the boy behind the counter struggled to smile through pimples and braces, while still managing to look older than the cadre of little hellions who were slurping and texting at the table by the window. So, I'm just sayin'… deduction does seem to stand on my side of the hunch.

Anyway, the French call cream "crème" because the French feel compelled, always, to have prettier words for things than everyone else.

But history tells us that no amount of linguistic one-upsmanship could rob the British of their love for the custard tart. And besides, how could any sound person not revel—along with the Brits and their penchant for heavily clotted veins—in the creaminess that inspired such fruity desserts as the *Norfolk Fool*, the *Devonshire Whitepot*, and the *Strawberry Mess*… fools and messes whipped up back in centuries when fruit was considered "unhealthy," so they boiled it down to mush to make it safer and softer to eat.

But I digress.

I came to sample the Crimson and Crème, a frozen custard dessert mixed with strawberries and bananas that they keep referring to here at Rusty's as a "Concrete"—a vivid image of what this thing will do to my insides—and such a harsher name than its French and British predecessors.

But I digress again.   So, let me just say...

really good stuff, man.

Cheese in the Garden of Eden

lasagna rolls from Victoria's,
and dinner salads from Victoria's

It's a small quiet jewel just off one of the more hidden lanes of Campus Corner in Norman—one of those little shoppy areas that sprout up in college towns and then eventually lose their character due to the creeping funk of Starbucks and the usual spread of Banana-this and Burrito-that chain stores. You know... the flashy and tasty blight of capitalism.

But Victoria's hangs in there, beating back the blight.

> Victoria's... where the polished and well employed eat, yet the hippies still run free.

> Victoria's... where the atmosphere is plain and sane, while on the walls, art school undergrads display the well-framed evidence of their continuing struggle with all the ways they were mistreated in front of their lockers in high school... so anxious they are to graduate from angst to full-blown madness.

> Victoria's... where the dinner salad—with its lemony-light dressing, fresh romaine, and shaved parmesan—deceives you, like Eden's serpent, into thinking, "This is healthy!" until the lasagna rolls arrive with their bubbling mounds of greasy white cheese... greasy white cheese with lightly browned edges that indicate some amount of time was spent bathing in a skillet lined with butter.

Sure, the menu made some mention of shrimp and spinach as being among the ingredients. However, they are but poor players upon this stage... each a mere piccolo and subtle bassoon in this oleaginous orchestra of pasta and pressed curds of milk.

Sweet and Salty

Dutch oven potatoes from Iron Starr

Sweet potatoes...
    earth-orange...
        baked into a soft,
            dark submission.

And I ordered a side of the fried onions and jalapeños to burn
the edges off the sweet.

You see the metaphor developing here? So, I'll extend it by
tacking on a margarita—a margarita with salt that I generously
spiked with a Sauza Gold mini I bought at Byron's on 23rd...
a mini I hid in my book-bag because I'm here alone today,
having hurt, for the third time this week, the best and most
beautiful thing in my sotting life.

C'mon... a book about you, Jim, won't be all culinary and
happy.

Truth is, I'm here killing time between an author-signing at a
library—where I sold one remaindered copy of my first book
to a 12-year-old for 5 dollars—and my daughter's 14th birthday
party at her mom's.

Brilliant... a bad fiancé and slightly buzzed father. What a
poetic combo. But you know? In my defense—sad as it may
be—I've come to believe there must've been a reason Jesus
ordered wine at the last supper.

You know...
    a little somethin'
        to take the edge
            off that last night.

Avocado in Three Movements

and my own guacamole

The Recipe

Your recipe for guacamole went with you, I'm afraid. LeAnn apologetically shook her head when I asked about this one. But the great green dip happens to be one of my specialities as well, and I've had a couple of opportunities to inflict it upon folks lately. I'll get to those stories in a minute.

Though I edit my ingredients on the fly for different occasions—like I edit my poems at readings when Baptists are present—my favorite version comes from years of observing the tenured hands of Lupe, the master of table-side guac at La Plazuela in Santa Fe.

First, roast an entire garlic bulb an hour or so before show time—a process that will leave the house reeking of its piquant perfume for days. Then, go ahead and wash the cilantro so it has some time to dry. (Wet cilantro sticks to the skin like farm pond leeches.)

Chop some onion. (And light a candle while you're at this if you cry at the end of Hugh Grant movies or when they sing the National Anthem at high school football games. It helps with the tears.)

Then dice a roma tomato... and do the same to a jalapeño. (But be sure to scrape out the seeds if your friends are from the North or are otherwise wimps.)

And, finally, slice the avocados in half... pop the pit... use a tablespoon to scoop out the sexy green flesh... throw in all above items... add big pinches of salt... squirt with lime juice... then get down to the grinding work.

A Rare Request

I recently had the rarefied privilege of making a toned down version of my guacamole for my daughter on the precarious occasion of her 14th birthday party.

Not to overplay this… but… for a 14-year-old to request anything—besides money—of a parent, is an unlikely convergence of the normally diametrical forces of adolescent cell division.

Anyway, she wanted it… said mine was the only guacamole she would eat. So, with no small amount of joy, I made it for her while she fought with her mom and commiserated with friends in the back yard.

Van Gogh's Favorite Colors

Joshua and Tiffany came over to break corn chip in the guacamole together and to drink from the cups of vodka and aged tequila…

> for these are the body
> and the blood as well.

To spend an indigo evening in June in the swirling glow of tiki torches and starlight, with a couple of folks who "get it," is gold in some kind of karmic bank, I'm sure… insurance against some amount of madness.

And in this moment of missing your friendship, Jim, as we gather with these new friends around candles and the great green dip, I'm reminded that Jesus did not weep over Jerusalem, but over the enemies of peace that clotted her yellow veins.

And so, as I bathe in the deep blue calm of this night, I think about that solemn preacher's kid of Holland and wonder if...

one or two more
    friends like these

might've spared
    his ear the razor...

maybe even his heart
    from the eternal sadness
        of that final bullet.

Strawberry and Banana

strawberry banana cake from Leo's

Nowadays, when I slip away to a meal of seared flesh and fat, it feels like I'm sneaking off for an illicit rendezvous with a gray-eyed mistress.

Honestly, I just don't eat the bloody stuff as much as I used to, Jim. And no matter who prepares it... whether smoked in hickory, mesquite, or maple for however many hours... it's never quite as tender as it used to be.

But when Leo's son sang about how his main ingredient is love, something of the brutal edge fell off the gristle and sinew. He patted me on the back and asked "How ya doin'?"

"Fine," I said.

He shaped a big ol' forefinger and thumb into a gun and pointed it at me from up by his cheek and shot back, with a hick'ry fire in his eyes, "Well... you fixin' to be a whole lot bettuh." The doctor had spoken.

Now... I know you brought me here for the famous strawberry banana cake at Leo's Barbecue. But anybody who's been once knows that a piece comes free with any meal you order. And even I can work out the finances on that deal.

So, not long after my basket o' spare ribs and baked beans showed up, Aunt Cookie dropped by with my yellow slice o' the good stuff. And... my friend... there were thick, real chunks of fresh strawberry and banana on top.

Something real in a world that often promises... but seldom delivers.

Flowers and Dust

grilled salmon from Cheever's

"Romantic Atmosphere..."

Restaurants lie, cheat, and kill for the reputation.

But does it come from the amount of money spent on
architects and interior decorators... or maybe from the whims
of self-appointed food critics? Or does it blossom from the
rich soil of simplicity... white tablecloths, black cloth napkins,
a fresh flower at every table, a spotless wine stem at every
place-setting?

I suppose if they turn the lights down low enough, almost any
place can fake it. But here at Cheever's—hidden away in one
of the many shadowy inner outbacks of Oklahoma City—a
part of the allure at least derives from almost a century of red
dirt and dust collecting in the mortar between the bricks of
the building.

It opened as a flower shop in 1927. And I'm wondering if it's
a trace of the good will that flowers intend that I'm tasting
now in my potato crusted salmon and the glass of white zin
that I ordered right up in the face of better taste.

Well... I know only this...

no amount of atmosphere and wine will feel romantic if the
one you share them with is not. So...

> a toast to my love...
> who most certainly is.

Pearl and Red

along with swirls from La Luna

Now... this is what I'm talkin' about. A frozen pearl and red party drink served in an 18-ounce carafe. A carafe, Jim. A medium-sized water pitcher.

With a thick circle of salt around the mouth, a lime wedge on the lip, and a panoply of different wines and liquors, this thing glows in the dark. It's enough to confuse a depressed Russian double-agent.

Seems like the waitress mentioned
                              Cherry Brandy...
                  Brandy...
        Vodka...
and Everclear, among several other things.

But, here,   half - way
    through
            my
      second   swirl,
I'm just not gonna remember what they were.

What is clearer though, is that these are good folks... good friends... who came to the table today. Some to honor you. And a few to help me celebrate the luscious debauchery and splendid idiocrity of my journey through your gastronomical dream.

Hell, Calvin even showed up—Norman's most famous paperboy-turned-movie-star—and caught three of us lubed up enough to buy a Transcript for three times what it's worth.

So!   A well-oiled toast...

To you, my good man!

And to these, my fellow sailors… with swirls held high…
who have been so gung-ho (or at least politely indulgent)…

Here's to those who wish us well,
and all the rest can go ta…

Ahh… forget it.
I just love ever'body!

An Expensive Cure

cheese bread from Pepperoni Grill

It floats up through the fog in my mind… some image from an old black and white Tarzan movie when Johnny Weissmuller parts the jungle's vines—or maybe he stepped through some waterfall—to the Great, and breathtakingly mysterious, Elephant Graveyard where all beasts heavy with trunk and ivory make their way to die.

Anyway, that's what I think of when mall doors swoosh open to a well-lit but ghostly space where figures move about clutching bright bags filled to the brim with self-improvement… such a spiritually barren place where something of the soul goes to die.

And you forced me to come here for cheese bread.

> Here where half the time half the wait-staff, and a manager half-managing, stood intently comatose beneath the shifting glow of the World Cup on a big screen in the bar.

> Here where I suffered through Bananarama singing "Venus" as one of the Badder parts of the Bad 80s pulsed and throbbed in cheap speakers.

> Here where I saw a Korean couple treat a Chicana waitress like crap for her lack of skill in English—a great way to get out of their tip.

But I will say that the thick layer of stretchy white cheese inside the crunchy dome of that soft white bread did live up to your promise. So warm. So soft. So mitigating. Almost.

And I believed the loud African waiter when he told us...
while wiping out water glasses... *Yeah, that cheese bread is what*
we all eat in the mornings here, back in the kitchen, to help cure our
hangovers.

Ribs and Stones

Just in from his walk through a cold summer rain in Taos, my friend and fellow poet, Navé, called me back on his cell and riffed on the Last Supper—a strange, unexpected gift neither one of us knew either one of us needed.

In a bit of a Marlon Brando, except clear enough to understand, he said,

> *I   have   always*
> > *been hungry   ...   hungry*
> *as a rib   sticking   out*
> > *of   an   abdomen ...*

> *I   ...   need   ...   food.*

And he went on without breathing. And I'd only called because he'd sent a cryptic email telling me I would receive a secret gift if I called him at this number. So I called it.

That's when he asked me, *What's on your mind... the most important thing to you right now?*

And I answered, *The Last Supper.*

And he said, *Here is your poem... your secret gift.* And, like I said, he went on without breathing...

> *This stone... let it be*
> > *this   stone...*
> *and I will suck on it*
> > *for a hundred   years.*

And he went on for another few minutes... brought me to eventual tears... tears I shed again now in this imperfect remembering of his immediate access to the pain in my request.

> *But I don't want it to be*
> *my last supper...*
> *I want   to eat   forever.*

These last honest words erupted from his own internal wilderness... a plea that sounded so much like yours there in those last few years of Hail Mary therapies and prayers.

.

The Story of the Day

cheese fries from Eskimo Joe's

"World Famous" gets thrown around in the food business—
from burger joints to bakeries—like "Instant Winner" does on
the envelopes of the Publishers Clearing House Sweepstakes.
And both are good indicators of when to walk away.

But I remember—as clearly as if it were only 20 years ago—
the moment I first believed Eskimo Joe's wasn't just yankin'
our collective chains when it comes to the claim.

One hot September, a friend and I drove up through the
Negev Desert on our way back to Jerusalem from Eilat—a
resort town on the Red Sea that feels a bit like Fort
Lauderdale. Somewhere along the western shore of the Dead
Sea, within smiling distance of Jordan, we stopped at a place I
can only describe as a KOA-meets-church-camp to try and
scare up some food—for we were great with hunger in the
land of King David's exile.

We were directed, in clear Hebrew and with a couple of hand
gestures, to a huge cafeteria filled with plywood tables and
teenagers who were obviously refugees from a nearby kibbutz.

Many of the details are foggy now... except for one.

When we were done, and I stood up to take my tray and
dishes to the kitchen, I turned around to the back of a t-shirt
that sported Eskimo Joe's famous slogan:

Stillwater's Jumpin Little
Juke Joint

There you have it.

Anyway, today my fiancée, my daughter, and I drove back roads—past no seas... save the big blue of a summer storm in the sky—to the Okie town of your schoolin'. We ate the cheese fries with grins almost as big as Joe's. We dipped them in the ranch dressing they serve with every order—to further harden the arteries.

There was much talk and Tic-Tac-Toe... much laughter and deep-fryer grease with melted cheese... such gooey love.

Capturing the Moment

My daughter sat with me in the now
of our cheese fries yesterday.
But that now is now a back then…
and will be forever.

And I have so many more
back thens with her
than nows anymore.

Her nows are filled with friends,
iPhones, and boy-problems now,
while her parents become back thens
that will take her decades to appreciate.

And if we all ever do luck our way into
the new nows of tomorrow,
I dream of a day when we'll all sit down
to a big fire with big glasses of wine
beneath fiery stars in a black velvet sky
and recount a lifetime of sacred nows
that are now all fuzzy back thens—

one big muddy roll in the misdemeanor
of nostalgia and its intoxicating allure.

We'll speak of a thousand back thens
in a long series of I remember whens…

      until they all finally alloy
            into one great bigger now.

Sauce Man

mango chicken from Misal

It's that yellow-orange sauce,
        speckled with spice,
                next to the saffron rice,
that makes the chunks of chicken superfluous...

makes me wish Ginger and LeAnn, Maddye and Will (the new boyfriend you didn't get to meet) hadn't been there with me at the table last night, so I could've licked the plate. A problem I have when it comes to great sauces.

Ashley was there too. But she lets me get away with it... and... actually... kinda likes it in a way that's not appropriate to detail for the purposes of this book.

Look... I mean only to illustrate how Misal's mango sauce sits on the verge of nectar status. And I felt that way even after I'd already been sipping their spicy-hot avocado-cilantro chutney through a little black martini straw. Another problem I have.

Anyway, we raised a glass of white zin, one martini, and two humongous brown bottles of Taj Mahal beer in your honor. And I did my best to be good and keep my tongue to myself.

Too Chany Meshiritas

and Cheshiritas

Today—because of you, Jim… and not because I make any money as a writer—it was my job to follow your wife over to the Cheshire's house, not far from yours, or mine, and drink sweet margaritas on a summer afternoon with a small group of hot mamas. That is… until some of the husbands and my fiancée arrived… after which they became fine women in the neighborhood.

And I'm only talkin' smack like this because of the Cheshirita's profound effect on one's ability to think clearly, like… for instance… now… as I begin to wonder what said fiancée will think when she reads this over coffee in the morning… not to mention the husbands when the book comes out.

Anyway, you spoke in a tone of fondness and respect when it came to your many memories of this socially lubricating drink. And I had four, my friend. And that's not counting the piña colada I'm fairly damn sure Alan made me there at the end of things. I even recall, vaguely, a Captain Morgan's Spiced Rum floater on top to boot.

But everything turned out fine, just like the last few parties you and I threw together. And Suzanne was kind enough to remind me where the front door had been… the one I could've sworn I'd walked in through only hours before.

Anyway, I'm home now… where I'm writing this and thinking what a great bunch of friends you had… and wondering if I'm gonna need to walk back over and get my car tomorrow.

Big Giblets

I know… I've got to back off the alcohol and coffee with all
that cream, or my expanding little sack of fat—

> the one that grows underneath the stomach muscles
> and always looks like the giblets from a giant chicken
> when Dr. Oz uncovers it on that rolling, stainless
> steel table on his show and then registers his deep
> concern for what the men of this country are doing to
> their bodies—

is going to begin to look like the ones on those guys who eat
the Pork Ribs Special once or twice a week at Applebee's and
then go home and scratch their stuff while watchin' the big
game on a threadbare couch with a cold and sweaty brewski.

Wise Decision

LeAnn's broccoli mushroom dip,
Kathy's homemade potato salad

I smelled it first, just inside the front door. Then I rounded
the corner and saw it simmering… bubbling and
smoldering… in a huge skillet on the stove.

LeAnn said it'd been about ten years since she'd made it last,
but I could tell when I leaned over it with my nose a few
inches away why you'd remembered it for your Last Supper.

I almost stuck a finger in for a taste, but I pulled back when
she told me the Frito Scoop had been your chip of choice and
then slid a bowl of 'em across the counter for me.

I don't know why, but I've gotten a bit ceremonious when it
comes to first bites of the foods you loved… crossing myself
over the chest if I'm alone… or only in my mind when I'm
with others. Such a fine line between ceremonious and
sanctimonious. That's why I peeled apart a fresh set of paper
plates when LeAnn pulled her stepmother's potato salad out
of the fridge. So many fine people doing so many fine things
for the cause, even when they're not quite sure what in the
world I'm up to.

And in light of these two dishes, I'd like to take this
opportunity to thank you, Jim, for this evening of mostly
vegetables. Your list has been pretty damned deep fried
and/or smothered in sauce so far. So I appreciate the break.

Oh and by the way, both items… abso-flippin-lutely delicious.
At one point I wanted to skip the chip and just wipe the
broccoli mushroom dip all over my face. But I worried LeAnn
might not see the compliment in that.

This

Tonight's lost supper hinged, of course, on LeAnn's dip and Kathy's potato salad. But the ongoing stream of sparkly mojitos LeAnn kept making from fresh mint growing in the garden, did broaden the evening's lamentous smile quite a bit.

We all glommed for a good while by the pool in those zero-gravity lawn chairs, back there in the yard you loved so dearly. And Gracie—the devoted dog you loved even dearlier—was curled up next to her reflection in the water.

And though those rumally mojitos are still, hours later, messin' with my suffixative and adjectivial skills somewhat, I wanted to tell you how at one point, through the porch door and windows, I saw your daughter and her new beau drift into the kitchen and stand over the broccoli mushroom dip with chips—their eyes rolling and closing in the broccoliness and mushroomy goodness of it. And for her… maybe even the spark of some distant memory.

In that moment a fleck of guilt lodged in the corner of my eye, and I cried—my face held away from Ashley and LeAnn. And I know you would've wanted me there this evening. But I also know you wanted…

hoped for…

were dying for…

more nights like this.

In My Mother's Home Town

The Blue Dome Diner's French toast

After a morning drive up Route 66, immersed in the insane green that stains Oklahoma hills after a series of midsummer rains...

> past the Round Barn in Arcadia and the Rock Café in Stroud...

> past the corporate biker gangs that would kill to go back to the authenticity, mushrooms, and free sex of the 60s...

a wayfarin' glutton will find the Blue Dome Diner somewhere on 2nd Street in downtown Tulsa.

I got your French toast with blueberries and a glass of chilled orange juice on the side—something to cut the wood-warping humidity that hangs inside the 90° plus-some heat. What wonderfully blue and French food in such a great little diner in such a culturally ambiguous town with such a dark and racially divided legacy. But I'm not telling you anything new.

Our poems received a warm reception at that one church here—a reception not in balance, however, with the few times we were snubbed by the hermetic literary community that holes up in isolated colonies scattered about these streets... a snobbery possibly related to the murky residue that seeped into the water supply from a century of Sooners, Boomers, and other bygone cheats and coots slowly gentrifying in a warm bath of old oil money.

But hey... what do I know?

Lattes in Purgatory

lattes from Shades of Brown

As I stared into the striations
of the steam-infused milk—
brown and bubbly white veins
in a barista's conceptualization
of a leaf... this barista's vision
carried to fruition in her own
special art foam—

I pondered one of my favorite things to happen upon in this
part of town: the young Oral Roberts University student.
Often they travel in pairs and sit at the table next to you,
writhing in their devout confusion over hormones, Holy
Bibles, and a fortune-teller who couldn't keep his eyes still...
or his accounts balanced. And they consume small vats of
caffeine to maintain their shaky certainty.

But who can blame them? Have you seen that statue on South
Lewis? Sixty some-odd feet of bronze praying hands shooting
skyward are hard to argue with. And thirty tons of piety can
come down on a soul with considerable influence. A piety, by
the way, the great evangelist had cast in Mexico and then
shipped to Tulsa, because Americans were charging too much.

Anyway... the ORU student is a beautiful thing to see,
because I lived for so long in a similar perplexity.

But now I've traded it for the only thing worse...

Poetry.

Sin Big

barbecue from Dink's

When I stepped inside Dink's, a few flies drunk on table scraps beat the hostess to the punch on greeting me. But soon enough she came after me n' the flies both, wavin' a menu in our faces.

She seated me at a table in the white-tiled back room across from four cowboys who smelled a bit of that which we were all about to partake.

One of them had a comb-over, spurs, and jeans tucked into boots. But the one closest to me had on a huge 10-gallon Stetson, a notably pink long-sleeve button-up shirt, and jeans tucked into almost knee-high black and white leather boots. Of course, the hat might've only been 5 gallons, but 10-gallon is all I've ever heard. Either way, my momma woulda whooped him up-side the head for not takin' that sweat-stained thing off at the table.

While we waited on combination plates piled high with every denomination of domesticated farm animal consumed by man, the cowboy with the spurs opened up a briefcase and pulled out a laptop. He pointed at the screen and mumbled something about cows and heifers to the one in the pink shirt who had trouble listening because he was busy texting on an iPhone.

Okay… okay… I know that's not what I came here for. And besides, Larry McMurtry'll tell you cowboys don't really exist anymore anyway. But you know how distracted I get. Anyway, I got the Lone Star Combination with the hot sausage and ribs… hot sausage because it's the one thing I miss most since I became a non-practicing vegetarian… and ribs because, if

I'm going to commit a mortal sin, I want to commit it all over my hands and face.

I'm tellin' you, Bub, you and your damn poem have waved more beef and pork in my face in the last two months than I have casually walked by in the last two years while on my way to another table. And I'm tellin' ya, it'd all better come off my abdomen as easily as the meat on this rib is comin' off the bone.

What Brings Us Here

my Dad's hot chili

I drove around the block a few times... locked the car... went back to check it... before I finally walked up and rang the doorbell. Geeze... it was like I'd come to pick up your ghost for the prom or something. But your mom opened up and helped me feel pretty comfortable pretty fast by showing me some old family photographs of you and your siblings with kids. Then, after some chitchat, the three of us went downstairs to eat.

First, we sat at the couch for nacho-cheese chips and some delicious ranchy-type dip your mom made. She told me it was always the first thing you asked for when you came to visit. And that launched us into storytelling a lot quicker than I thought we'd get to it. To be honest, we also laughed more than I thought we would.

Your dad brought his hot chili to the table in a huge aluminum stew pot and dipped it out into bowls. You know it's chili-time in Oklahoma when there's a big round platter close at hand that's loaded with grated cheese, chopped onions, salsa, and a bunch o' Fritos. Hot dang! I have so many great memories of this taste—so many wonderful sunlit-picnic, Sunday-go-to-meetin', hot-afternoons-in-the-park histories with this dish. And your dad's knocks it out of the stadium, man.

He worried it wasn't spicy enough because your mom wasn't adding ketchup to her bowl to cool it down a bit—like she's prone to do, apparently. It was workin' for me though.

And so, this is how a person, I guess, falls into a new kaleidoscopic world of talking cats and rabbits... or... say...

how a poem—a single poem—can bring a man into the home
of a good friend's parents… the home he grew up in… the
good friend who lost his life to the contaminated fallout of an
industrial century… to eat chili with his wounded parents…
parents who'd already grieved one good child before…

so we could all try to remember

the better parts of things.

They Are the Brown Sugar of the Earth

my mom's pecan pie

All the things our mothers make us. All the days… from day one… they feed us. And I'm just now thinking about how little we take into account the sheer weight in pounds of all the food they prepare for us in our lifetimes.

How do we thank them for the absurdity of their sacrifice… the biology of their love… without which, not only would *we* die, but most species would cease to be?

I know you had differences of opinion with your parents. But I broke chip and dip with the salt of the earth tonight at your childhood home—the good people who hold the world together while the crazy people like you and me try to find some way to tell the good people that the survival of the human race depends upon us both… both kinds of people.

Your mother's pecan pie vaulted me into a world inhabited by my grandma and great-grandmother in Cyril, Oklahoma. I'm sure my poems and books would've scared them to death. At the same time, I'd've had nothing to worry about, because they never would've read them. Not out of a lack of love for me, but because they'd've had beets to pickle, tomatoes to can, and plums to preserve and jar.

I mean… somebody had to make the lye soap after the hog-killin's. And we all know poets are good-for-nothin's when it comes to cookin' n' scrubbin' the necessities of life. When Christmas-time came around your house, who was gonna make the pecan pie… you? What good's a lawyer at adding just the right amounts of brown sugar and corn syrup? A more precise science has never been practiced.

I tried to bake a pecan pie once. It was a goopy and glorious disaster. But your mom's was as good as any I've ever tasted. And I'm only just now beginning to see how home-pickled beets and pecan pies are among the quotidian miracles of our earthly existence that we so often take for granted... until impending death throws life in our faces

and we finally sit down
to write the poem about it.

No Recipes for These Territories

*my great grandmother's green beans
and her apple butter to smear*

Great grandmothers seldom wrote these things down. They
didn't follow recipes. They cooked the food that was available.

They grew the green beans out back... picked 'em... then
threw 'em in a pot to boil. Flavor came from whatever was to
hand. Always salt and pepper. Sometimes ham hocks. Or...
according to your mom, Jim, your great grandmother's
involved a generous amount of bacon grease. What's not to
like about that?

They didn't *buy* butter. They churned it. They didn't run to the
store for Mott's Apple Sauce. They peeled and cored apples...
real apples... stewed 'em in big pots... added cinnamon, some
sugar, maybe a little nutmeg if they had it around.

And they didn't stand with hands on hips while stooped over
a cookbook. They stood next to their mothers with their
hands deep into the business of cookin', because the
continuation of the species depended on it.

Now'days, when the strange and rare impulse comes over us
to actually cook our own food—as opposed to ordering
Chinese takeout—we go to recipes dot com and have a
terrible time narrowing down our 35,000 options to the one
we're gonna prepare, then start making the grocery list.

And I didn't mean for this to turn into a sermon illustration,
    but I am beginning to feel a primal need
        to get my hands
            back deep
                into the business of things.

Forsooth...

an Economic Sonnet

While I take this long sybaritic roll
in the mud of epicurean excess—
I've tried to keep in mind...
with wobbling degrees of success...

that it is, no doubt, my country
which accords me this surplus—
my country and its somewhat
myopic view of progress.

So here's a shout-out to Wall Street...
the Fannie Maes and Freddie Macs...
the Bear Stearns, the AIGs,
and the Goldman Sachs...

may we live on... and without duress...
in the beautiful mud of this beautiful mess.

White or Wheat

on bread from the County Line

Present—
Carol, Dorothy,
Devey, and Sandra

Only five disciples made it to the last of
the lost suppers to be held in the home
state. But the group was so right for the
part—a tiny crew of the great ladies of Oklahoma poetry
who'd loved you, supported you, published you, and mourned
you deeply.

The loaf came in thick slices... half white... half wheat. And,
as you would know, a loaf that goes both ways made this
bunch feel right at home. We passed the basket around to
each disciple, broke and buttered our bread, and then...
someone raised a cup.

We all followed.

And in a hush uncharacteristic of these reveling bandits and
literary thieves we intoned
"For Jim"

One cup bled with the deep maroon of pinot noir. One bottle
held the harvest of amber ale. And one glass required iced tea
with a slice of lemon because the blood of the sacrifice—
namely Chivas Regal Scotch—had been a bit rough on the
system in her earlier years.

The Eucharist is what it is.

If Jesus had been a songwriter,
    he'd've served pretzels and whiskey.

108

If he'd been a Baptist...
      dry toast and grape juice.

But whatever bread we break...
      and whichever cup we take...

            we do it in love
                and remembrance.

The Basic Ingredients

waffles from Original Pancake House

Billy Crockett flew into Dallas from Austin just to share this meal—a gesture that no longer seems unusual when it comes to your Last Supper list. Over the last month or so, I've seen people commit amazing acts of uncertainty folded into an overriding kindness and love for you.

This morning, though, you brought two friends together to drink from the sacred cup of beginnings… a cup Billy and I shared many times many years ago: the coffee here at the Original Pancake House on Beltline in Dallas.

We called it, affectionately, the shit. And we agreed again, this time around, that it's still the shit. And you know? We needed this cup of it, because we've been through some of it together over the last few years.

Artistic friendships, historically, flash with the lightning of passionate discourse, righteous disagreement, and then… if all goes well… repair and resolve, because productive artistic friendships are rare and, more often than not, the stuff of deep survival.

Hemingway and Fitzgerald almost killed each other before they killed themselves. Tolkein and C.S. Lewis fought like barbarians over religion and pints of ale at the Bird and Baby pub in Oxford. Pissarro and Monet. Laurel and Hardy.

I'm not sure where Billy and I fall in that spectrum. And I can't say I know what it means to call someone a "best" friend. How about "critical," "foundational," maybe "artistically volcanic." But always inspirational.

110

The waffle you brought me here for was not all these things. Maybe fabulous. Maybe got-dang delicious. Maybe even one of the best I've had. But not "artistically volcanic," I'm afraid.

The waffle did, however, bring us to the table in celebration of friendship. And to serve as an element of such a communion, is surely a high calling for eggs, milk, and flour.

Never Know

07/25/2010
9:33 PM
30092

Table 23

Server: Jesus

This receipt from breakfast
might make a case
for diacritical markings
above certain vowels.

But I know it's cause
for keeping your eyes open.

Proof
that you never know
where or when
he's going to offer you
the bread and wine.

Las Vegas:
The Last Leg of the Lost Suppers

*For me, Vegas is a vacation from being
overinhibited, in the highly overinhabited
yet uninhabitable city of complete
uninhibition.*

~Tammy Bloemzaken

We'll Always Have Paris

The four of us met in Paris.

> Well… the lobby.

More specifically… a roulette table in the lobby of Paris Las Vegas where Ashley was in the process of winning back the twenty bucks she'd lost at The Mirage earlier in the afternoon.

Matter of fact? She walked away from the whirling black and red rush ten dollars in the good. My baby'd beat Vegas, and we made our getaway without a single shot fired.

❀ O ❀

LeAnn had flown in from Oklahoma City the night before… and, Jim… I've gotta tell you… few people caught the spirit of this last supper pilgrimage better than she. Not that it was a "sacrifice" to come spend a day or two in Vegas. But she saw it… the sideways tribute I was trying to pay. And she not only put up with my lunacy… she made many parts of it possible.

To even out the numbers, but not the odds, Don took on the hell of morning traffic in L.A., and then the Mojave Desert, just to break butternut squash ravioli with me. He's a good friend and a big part of the reason we were all here.

Let me back up a hair.

When I first got what I thought was this cute idea in my head, to eat my way through your last supper, I didn't realize that your poem on the subject had left out one critical detail. It said, simply, "butternut squash ravioli from Olives." I saw it as code-speak for Olive Garden. And I knew where a couple of those were. No problem. Right? Until… one night… after I'd already gorged myself half-way down your list, we had

LeAnn over to, first, ply her with margaritas and then, finally, reveal what I was up to… or… that to which I was up.

Midway through her third rita, I have to say she seemed quite amenable to, if not amused by, my presentation of the project. That is… until… I mentioned this one item I wasn't sure about. That's when she gagged on a big sip and choked out, *Oh no… not "Olives" as in Garden… "Olives" as in… the Bellagio in Las Vegas.*

Now we were all choking on third margaritas, and I was, already, trying to devise a scenario that would get me out of the deal that I just then realized I had struck with the Devil— because… Vegas is clearly one of his major transitional points for people who grew up Baptist.

Thoughts went off like fireworks:

> *I don't have the money for that.*
> *I can't fly.*
> *It's two days' drive!*
> *Where would I stay?*
> *Do they have a Motel 6 out there?*
> *And how much would that cost… considering the Motel 6 would even have slot machines and some kind of dorky "We'll Leave a Light on for Ya!" theme?*

So the next day I called my friend Don Dorsey.

Don… who designed, produced, and directed the music and fireworks for the Golden Gate Bridge's 50th Birthday Party.

Don… who designed, produced, and directed a one-time massive video projection onto the famous fountains in front of the Bellagio for the "Vanishing Point Game"—some super

115

high-tech puzzle for mega-geeks that was backed by Microsoft and AMD.

Don... who—when meeting with the head execs of Disney one time (including the CEO, Michael Eisner himself) about the dream and design of the Millennium Show that would run at the Epcot Center in Disney World for ten years—actually said, when some young buck jumped up and passionately blurted, *The sky's the limit!*

Well then... we're gonna need a bigger sky.

This... is the friend I called for help. And he, of course, told me:

Well... you know...

long pause... my shoulders drooped...

you're going to have to do it.

Dammit. There were any number of other people I could've called. And I chose Don.

He was...
however...
right.

So the four of us gathered there by the roulette table and made our way with smiles and soft laughter—yet with a muted sense of the mission—across Las Vegas Boulevard to the Bellagio.

Crossing Las Vegas Boulevard being…

the last great test for the heroes

in our mythguided journey.

Layover at the Sleeping Dog Tavern

Let me back up even further...

Santa Fe serves as the first stopping point on all my trips of a westward nature. Heading into downtown on Old Pecos Trail or St. Francis, as I've done once or twice a year since I was two, feels like a homecoming every time. And these days, as soon as I find a place to park the car, we aim straight for the glowing hearth of the Sleeping Dog Tavern—a quiet little den on the bottom floor of the Plaza Mercado.

Gustavo, friend and manager, takes such good care of us. Last night, at the tail-end of our butt-numbing drive, he brought Ashley her Cuba Libre swimming with extra rum and a margarita for me "con mucho oro" ... "mas tequila." Both Spanish for "strong and happy" ... kind of.

His kindness reminds me how Leona once wet a napkin and told me to lean over the counter of her small tamale stand in Chimayó, just so she could wipe a drop of queso off my orange t-shirt like a pinch-hit grandma.

Or the way Carlos offered us each a chocolate truffle after brunch this morning... truffles to help us celebrate an anniversary at Luminaria in the Inn at Loretto... truffles that never showed up on the check or the room bill upon departure.

The same way that Gabe, the bartender at the Sleeping Dog, just yelled from the ice bin to make sure I have enough coffee to fuel today's poem and the rest of our trip.

And all these great folks have me wondering if—when I hit the madness of Las Vegas Boulevard tomorrow and check into the Paris resort—anyone in that town will give a desert-rat's ass that I don't I like my margaritas too sweet.

So, I tell Gustavo...

> *If they mistreat me out there,*
> *I'll be back... for the cure...*
> *on my way home.*

Mornings with Coffee at Mon Amí...

Where the palm trees
stand like frightened step-children
in the middle of Las Vegas Boulevard

and shake out their quivering fronds
in an early morning breeze
as they prepare for another day
of carbon monoxide's fury
and the flaying scorch
of Nevada's mid-day sun.

Where gay couples
from the bulge of the Bible Belt
come to escape the flames
of religion's righteous scorn

so they can drink their mimosas
and eat their Eggs Florentine
in the relative peace and quiet
of Vegas's orgy of humanity
that views their plaid shorts
and white canvas deck shoes
as little more than quaint...
        if not a tad boring.

Where brunettes
in cotton dresses short enough
to flash a decent-sized chunk
of a jiggling left butt cheek
with every other uncertain step

wobble by on the sidewalk
in gold high heels and black sunglasses
in search of a Starbucks 'r something
because they never even bothered
going back to the room last night
n' some caffeine 'r something
will help 'em push on through
to the next Happy Hour.

Where men of a certain ripeness
jog by in tiny Speedo running shorts
and leave nothing of the shocking
dark prune of their torsos
to the imagination.

Where, two tables over,
the middle-aged couple from Jersey
speak loudly to their Mexican-American waiter
because he has a slight accent
and must, therefore, be deaf.

The Usual Stuff…

Like the low-flow toilet
in the expensive 29th floor room
that didn't fancy the last customer

so when you take your turn
it slowly pushes the water
up towards its lip because

its thinkin' about making you pay for his sins.

Like the "Pool Closed" sign
that greets you at the iron gate
and makes you grit your teeth
when you question the attendant
who tells you it's because someone
threw up in the bright shiny water
trying to swim off the morning's hangover
and you think but do not say, well,
it was a pretty damn expensive room
so don't you think a well-trained staff
could've cleaned it up
by late afternoon?

Like the guys in red t-shirts
that read "GIRLS DIRECT TO
YOUR DOOR IN 20 MINUTES"
who stand on every other street corner
and smack rolled up color catalogues
of the local nude fare on their forearms
while they try to get enough

of your attention to shove
a copy into your hand…

and all this in spite of the beautiful
woman holding your hand who somehow
fails to send enough of a signal
to their reptilian brains that I just might
have already found what I'm looking for.

Like the hotel handyman who carries on
a loud conversation with the espresso machine
behind the counter of the Coffee Express
where your daily writing session
is already not quite working out
because of the airportish atmosphere

and then he has to go ahead
and pound the counter with his fist
as he shouts a few obscenities
before he storms off to retrieve
some other damned tool

at which point you are, at least,
grateful for the break.

Like Les Toilettes…
      in Le París hotel…
with a looped CD playing inside them
that instructs peers and poopers alike
how to properly say in French, things like:

Has anyone seen my panties?

Does the Little Chapel of the Pines take a check?

I shaved my legs for this?

Is that an éclair in your pocket… ?

Can I buy you a drink, or do you just want the money?

and the ever useful…

I'm never drinking again.

But no… wait a minute…

I actually enjoyed this whole private,
yet strangely public, moment.

Viva la Noise

There's just no quiet in Vegas

~Barry Manilow

Vegas has a musical soundtrack that pounds like a perpetual movie score running in its background. It assaults you in every casino... stays with you all the way through every hotel. It even follows you outside and down the sidewalk, pumping out of bridge columns and from the sides of buildings... an endless noise in a Technicolor surround-sound world that also pulses out of rolled-down car windows, lest you have a toneless moment between brief distances.

One mutant genre overlaps another with every step in this dazzling Xanadu where liquid crystal advertisements of nice asses in fishnet stockings appear to float unattached in the air around your head... any and every thing imagined to keep us in a suspended state of believing that this time...

we will beat the odds.

Though I will say that this afternoon, lost in some anonymous lobby, I thought I heard a whole verse of the Doobie Brothers' song "What a Fool Believes."

I felt a strange hope in even the hint of such a great tune. But...

as it turns out...

it was just The Mirage.

Down

A weekend in Vegas without gambling and drinking is just like being a born-again Christian.

~Artie Lange

At casino level, I walked by in awe of the tourist's ability to stand on bad shoes in collar-pullingly long lines for Expensive Tickets to see Cheap Trick... or... a chance to overeat at a buffet where none of us will know when to walk away from the table any better than we do from Blackjack or the hypnotic spin of the Roulette wheel.

Anyway, these lines drove us—being the misanthropes we are—down the boulevard to the low-rent district of Excalibur and the Luxor where, for instance, the lobby of New York New York felt like a Disneyland-scale sports bar—a thing ten-times as terrifying, at least to me, as Freddy Krueger ever dreamed of being in yet another bad sequel.

We walked back out the doors of the MGM Grand the moment we walked in and saw a glowing movie-poster-sized sign for Starbucks with a big green arrow pointing off into the growing darkness—just one of many possible gateways to hell in this town.

But it's not as if any hotel in Vegas is much more than a theme-airport with a nice yet thin veneer and a good number of slot machines.

However, I feel it only fair to mention that the end of our particular line brought us to Mandalay Bay where we finally felt weak enough to have to eat something. And this is when we happened onto Hussong's. Their wild mushroom version of Queso Fundido caught our attention on the menu. But let's be honest here, any place with big letters on its sign that read:

Less Ice
More Tequila

I mean, c'mon…

Besides, I'm a great appreciator of restaurants that include an educational element along with their culinary offerings.

I know it seems a guy with my special problem would already have some kind of grip on the history of the margarita. But I reveled in the news—however unreliable—that a bartender in the dust-choked border town of Ensenada created the drink for a beautiful woman… Margarita Henkel, the daughter of the German Ambassador to Mexico… back in October of 1941.

His name? Don Carlos Orozco. And in the history of civilization, so overrun with Huns, Khans, and Hitlers, he should be remembered as someone who fought to make the world a better place.

It matters not that some believe the woman was Rita Hayworth, whose given name was Margarita Carmen Cansino.

It matters only that Don Carlos imagined a better mix for the future…

   a mix of tequila, Damiana, and lime over ice…

   a future held in the humble vessel of a salt-rimmed glass.

Up

For the sake of balance, we explored uptown as well. Caught a whiff of Jimmy Buffet in the Flamingo. Made note of a fairly public penis on a statue in front of Caesar's Palace... a very white, somewhat unimpressive, and very lonely penis on the sidewalk in a town that obviously harbors a bias for the bare breasts and buttocks of more finely sculpted women. A bias, granted, that I share... at least to the extent that when it comes to the human form, women surpass men in both geometry and grace by immeasurable bounds.

Seeing Harrah's and Casino Royale from out on the sidewalk seemed sufficient enough. Once again the penchant for excruciating music pushed us on our way.

Just beyond the noise though, lie *The Venetian* and the *Wynn*— voted the two most likely resorts to spot God gambling on a rare but much needed vacation from followers. God... the only being in the universe with luck enough to, maybe, win at Keno. And though some might be tempted to think of him as a good candidate for The Palms, it turns out he lacks the Hollywood credentials to get in.

All glitz and glamor aside, what you're really after here hides in the heart of the *Wynn*. Look for the winding—yes, winding—escalators and let them carry you to Parasol Down, a little bar on the lower level. Parasol Up is fine if you're frightened by curving escalators. But, in this situation—and in the face of everything you learned in Sunday School—Down is better. For there... on a parasol-flocked patio, beside a pond-like pool with a huge waterfall at the far end... sit a few small tables in the shade where a waitress, in an even smaller skirt, will bring you... if you ask nicely... their Smoky Margarita—a little splash of perfection that comes with an even littler splash of Crema de Mezcal in a tiny terra cotta fingerbowl on the side.

Pour it in.
Let it percolate
down through the ice and tequila.

And lick the little bowl
when no one
is looking.

Conjecture

Las Vegas is Everyman's cut-rate Babylon.

~Alistair Cooke

You loved this greasy town... this flaky Utopia... the few times you got to visit in the last few years.

And I can't help but think how
different it would be, how strange,
if all of life was this dazzling,
this sparkling, this freakishly fun.

~Jim Chastain

In this town, a man missing an arm doesn't stand out. In this town, a man with cancer is only dying a little faster than the drunks, pimps, and gambling addicts stumbling all around him. In this town, a man wandering among the beeps and dings, the excited screams for the occasional winner at craps, and the twirling glow of slot machines, can revel in the suspension of time's normal pace. He can steal a few extra days... even if they're only imaginary.

Las Vegas turns women into men
and men into idiots.

~Benjamin "Bugsy" Seigel

This town's heart beats with the blood of its father... a father whose bipolar passions and lunatic temper planted the seeds for its buzzy and twitchy disquiet that blooms in a seductive neon angst. Yes...

Vegas is a gangster with a big heart.

It was engineered to make money. But it genuinely wants you to relax, forget about your pain, and have a damn good time while you're losing it.

Man, I really like Vegas.

~Elvis Presley

It's what you wanted.
It's what we're all after here…

to spend a few sleepless days in the isolated purgatory-like dimness of hell's luxurious lounge.

And it's shocking how pink it all is. Even more shocking that a hit man for the mafia would be so into flamingos. But, from what I understand, pink was the first color of the first feather to show up here in the Mojave Desert.

Las Vegas: all the amenities of modern society in a habitat unfit to grow a tomato.

~Jason Love

… and Good Luck

Las Vegas is the only town in the world whose skyline is made up neither of buildings, like New York, nor of trees, like Wilbraham, Massachusetts, but signs.

~Tom Wolfe

The roulette table has a digital sign up at the head that posts the last fifteen or so results of the wheel. It offers a clear picture of the past. But as Don explained, it supplies little more than a thumb-sucking kind of comfort where the future is concerned. Yet, in spite of that, eyes look up from a dwindling stack of chips and stare at the red and orange LEDs as if they hold some message… some hint as to where to drop the next five.

Apparently, eons of trial and error have not convinced us that nothing predicts—with any measurable accuracy—which chamber the spinning cylinder of a six-shooter will stop on. Much like you learned over time, Jim, that no amount of medical conjecture—no matter how well educated the guessing may be—can rig the roulette wheel in our DNA.

Signs. Signs of hope. Signs of progress. Some arrow. Some dotted line. Any damn divination of what damn direction to go next… we eventually learned to ignore.

Las Vegas is so full of signs, a person locks up in the neon confusion of it all. Good suggestions, for which nightclubs have the sexiest girls, fall out of the sky, littering the sidewalks and escalators.

Which Cirque du Soleil should we go to? I don't know. Walk into any hotel and attend whichever one is there. If not… settle for Cher.

꩜ O ꩜

Anyway… I had a good time in Vegas, my friend… in spite of what my letters to you may sound like. But it did help solidify my distrust of signs. Or… let me put it another way: it helped me let go of their hazardous allure.

The old bastard Bukowski would tell us that the horse behind Gate 3 may very well pull it out at the line… but to bet your savings on it?

That's when he'd go quiet…
      take another puff on a cheap cigar…
          then mutter…

                Good luck, baby.

Culmination

butternut squash ravioli from Olives

Alright...
I've put this off as long as I can.

Truth is...
this entire chapter
consists of things I wrote
in order to avoid writing
about the very last
of the Lost Suppers...

a strangely prolific version of writer's block.

I didn't want the odyssey to end.

It's a rare and wonderful year when a writer knows exactly
what he should be working on. Whether or not I'm
succeeding hasn't mattered in the least. I needed to talk to
you. And these letters were how I needed to do it.

However... now that I'm here... I'm faced with the quandary
of having no idea what to say about perfection.

For the poet, stumbling into the most beautiful woman in the
world would be like staring straight into the sun for a fraction
of a second too long. And trying to write about it afterward
would be like trying to drive from Vegas back home to
Oklahoma... still blind from the experience.

This is where the last leg of the lost suppers has left me.

When the best laid plans of mice or men go much, much
better than either the mice or the men could have imagined, it
makes a part-time pessimist nervous.

The place, Olives, was immaculate. And in spite of how the hostess must hear a good story or five every day, she seemed to believe mine and worked hard to get us a fabulous table by the marvelous windows.

While waiting for the fabulous table, an exceptional bartender shook us up some equally exceptional Cable Cars, Martinis, and Margaritas.

Once at the fabulous table, the spectacular Bellagio show of fountains and light exploded just outside the marvelous windows by our fabulous table. Even our waitress was exotically sweet. And when the second round of equally exceptional drinks arrived, the eclectic yet perfect gathering of the four of us—without suggestion or provocation— reverently raised our four exquisite glasses…

                                                    to you.

Like I said, Jim, the perfection of the moment was unnerving.

So, when the "Butternut Squash Tortelli" (that, I will admit, did look an awful lot like ravioli) appeared before me, I crossed myself—seeing as I consider myself a Catholic whenever I fly and… now… am remembering you over a rapturous meal at a fabulous table by marvelous windows with equally exceptional drinks and eclectic yet perfect gatherings of friends.

I crossed myself… welled up… with throat-clenching yet discreet sobs… hid my face while Ash grabbed my hand under the table…

                    and was finally able to say…

                                    goodbye.

One Last Big One

I almost came to expect pleasant surprises from friends and folks who had known you. Some small amount of word about my trippy little trip through your dream of a last supper got around I guess, and they began to show up at the gatherings.

They came to love some of the lattes and lettuce wraps you had loved... and to raise their Swirls and Cheshiritas to that.

Some offered me rooms to stay in when you required that I hit the road. Others shot me simple emails of appreciation and encouragement that helped more than I can explain in an acknowledgements page.

You see... for someone of my budgetary status, I blew a good bit of my ignominious fortune on this pilgrimage.

I'm not bitter. I don't feel a single waffle's-worth of regret. I'd even go as far as to say I've had one of the better times of my life over the months it took. But I am staring at a lip-scrunching hole in my wallet. And that's why I feel the need to mention one last, big, pleasant surprise that arrived with the pleasant surprises of Don driving from L.A. and LeAnn flying all the way from OKC just to join in on this last, last meal.

The one last big one was a blinking light on the phone in LeAnn's hotel room. She had a message to check in with the concierge at the Bellagio when we went over for dinner. So, when the time came, we headed out an hour early for her to look into that while the rest of us went on to Olives to make the plea for a special table.

It took her long enough that we were forced to go ahead and sit at the bar for a first round. Such sacrifices abounded throughout the long months of this culinary safari.

The ice in our glasses had shrunk somewhat by the time she came 'round. But she brought with her a small colorful box. In it was this note:

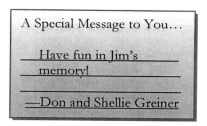

A Special Message to You…

Have fun in Jim's
memory!

—Don and Shellie Greiner

And under the note was a gift card that covered most of the dinner.

The amount would be inappropriate to mention. The impact, however… I hope will not be.

I'd set aside quite a bit of dough for this meal. It was the end of the line, and I had every intention of doing it right. So, let's just say, as far as the first level of impact, that I suddenly felt more secure when it came to gas money to get home.

The higher level, though, was less quantifiable.

People love you, Jim. Still.
    Your memory…
        your heart…
and the incredible way you carried yourself through the valley of the shadow of an impossible situation.

Their love and generosity continue to mess with me… in good ways—good ways that are very difficult for a recovering cynic to deal with as I try to wrap up whatever the hell it is I'm doing here.

Nonetheless, here is where the whole of this year has brought
me... on knees... head down... and as hokey as it may be:

Live the life you've been given.
    Not someone else's.
Only... throw in a few wild,
    unexpected colors, like
Electric Lime or Atomic Tangerine... or
    maybe Jazzberry Jam or Jungle Green.

Be who you were made to be.
    Not someone else.
Only... keep 'em guessing
    when you can.

Love the ones you love.
    And not too many other elses.

Love them with all you've got.
    And yet be kind to the other elses
        when they deserve it.

And finally...

    Live... Be... and Love...

        right up to the messy end...

            and then get on outta here...

                when it's time to go.

Stepping Back

It's time to walk away, Jim…
that moment in the movie
when the music swells up
like it's trying to say something
and so you know the credits are about to roll.

The camera's pulling back on the zoom now
to some wide angle… maybe panning over
a vast Arizona landscape along Route 66.

Wheels are rolling me back home
in the hum of inevitability
where I will open the door
and air out the stale classroom
for students, yet again, and only

because I love them more
than I hate the institution.

Well… that…
and the fact that I'm outta money.

I'd hoped for something profound
here at the end.

But I can't stand it
when a book sounds
like it's striving for that.

So

                    I guess

I will say

Thank you,
my friend...

and goodnight.

Author Bio:

Nathan Brown is a musician, photographer, and award-winning poet from Norman, Oklahoma. He holds a PhD in *Creative and Professional Writing* from the University of Oklahoma and teaches there as well. Mostly he travels now, though, performing readings and concerts as well as speaking and leading workshops in high schools, universities, and community organizations on creativity, creative writing, and the need for readers to not give up on poetry.

He has published six books: *My Sideways Heart* (2010), *Two Tables Over* (2008)—Winner of the 2009 Oklahoma Book Award, *Not Exactly Job* (2007)—a finalist for the Oklahoma Book Award, *Ashes Over the Southwest* (2005), *Suffer the Little Voices* (2005)—a finalist for the Oklahoma Book Award, and *Hobson's Choice* (2002).

Released in the spring of 2010, Nathan's new album of all-original songs, *Gypsy Moon*, is his first musical project to come out in over a decade.

His poems have appeared in: *World Literature Today*; *Concho River Review*; *Blue Rock Review*; *Sugar Mule*; *Di-verse-city* (anthology of the *Austin International Poetry Festival*); *Blood and Thunder*; *Wichita Falls Literature and Art Review*; "Walt's Corner" of *The Long-Islander* newspaper (a column started by Whitman in 1838); *Oklahoma Today Magazine*; *Blueberry Rain and Chocolate Snow*; *Windhover*; *Byline Magazine*; *Blue Hole: Magazine of the Georgetown Poetry Festival*; *Christian Ethics Today*; *Crosstimbers*; and *Poetrybay.com*… as well as in two anthologies: *Two Southwests* (Virtual Artists Collective, Chicago) and *Ain't Nobody That Can Sing Like Me: New Oklahoma Writing* (Mongrel Empire Press).

For more info, and to order books, go to: brownlines.com

CPSIA information can be obtained
at www.ICGtesting.com
Printed in the USA
FFOW03n0933021213
2533FF